THE COTSWOLDS

THE COTSWOLDS

Text by
ROBIN WHITEMAN
Photographs by
ROB TALBOT
Foreword by
JILLY COOPER

RIZZOLI
NEW YORK

Colour separations by Newsele Litho Ltd
Filmset by Deltatype, Ellesmere Port
Printed and bound in Italy by L.E.G.O., Vicenza

Half title page: Great Tew, Oxfordshire
Title page: Hidcote Combe, Gloucestershire
Overleaf: Broadway, Hereford and Worcester

ACKNOWLEDGMENTS

Robin Whiteman and Rob Talbot would like to thank everyone who so willingly gave their time to guide them around the properties and sites. They particularly wish to acknowledge the generous co-operation they received from the National Trust, Severn Region and Wessex Region, and the Cotswold Farm Park in allowing them unrestricted access to their properties over an entire year. Many individuals and organizations were of tremendous help notably: Lady Ashcombe and Sudeley Castle Ltd; Stephen Bird, Keeper of Local History, and Denis G. Easterby, Director of Leisure and Tourist Services, Bath City Council; Tom Burr, Regional Information Officer of the National Trust, Wessex Region. For the National Trust, Michael and Sue Jessup (Snowshill Manor); Nigel and Doreen Wilson (Chedworth Roman Villa); Bob Parsons (Newark Park); Paul Nicholls (Hidcote Manor Garden); Mrs Porter and Mrs Bateman (Horton Court); Mr and Mrs Justice (Dyrham Park); Mr Greenhalf (Hailes Abbey). Also, the Rev. Canon J. A. Lewis (Parish Church of St John the Baptist, Cirencester); Mr K. Gledstone (Rockness House, Nailsworth); Mr D. W. Newman (Bradley Barn Farm, Wotton-under-Edge); Mr A. V. Nicholls (The Old Smithy, Lower Swell); Joe Henson (Cotswold Farm Park); Seamus Stewart (Robert Dover's Games Society); John Jones (Longlands Farm, Chipping Campden); John Humphries (Ram Inn, Wotton-under-Edge). Special thanks go to Barbara Morley, Regional Information Officer of the National Trust, Severn Region, for all her help and encouragement.

CONTENTS

FOREWORD
by Jilly Cooper

We have now lived in the middle of the Cotswolds, the *haute* Cotswolds you might almost say (much of which is designated as an Area of Outstanding Natural Beauty), for four and a half years. Of course I had often visited the area in the past. During my courting days in Oxford one was often nipping off to Minster Lovell in the back of some undergraduate's sports car for lunch at the Swan, or enjoying bibulous picnics on the fringe of an elm-ringed (alas, no longer) village cricket ground in places rejoicing in such romantic names as Bourton-on-the-Water or Shipton-under-Wychwood. My parents, too, regularly came to the Cotswolds for a few days each year, staying at the Bay Tree at Burford where the food was so delicious and plentiful that one always put on at least seven pounds. Sometimes, to shed some of this weight, I would accompany them on long walks over the rolling hills enoying the endless song of the skylarks and the bleatings of hundreds of fat sheep as they grazed their fields down to carpet-pile texture, surrounded by mile upon mile of beautiful, neat, mellow, dry-stone walls.

Now all the enchantments of the Cotswolds are literally on my doorstep. The sun-welcoming stone of the houses in the sleepy villages, the ravishing churches, the astonishing variety of views and aspects that can be enjoyed from so many different vantage points in the often steep, dramatic wooded valleys. Views broken up by great beech plantations, Rowland Hilder-like tree clumps and the ever-present grazing lands. Then there are the wild flowers growing in abundance in secret places, the tumbling streams, crystal clear, so quickly converted to raging torrents by the fickle Cotswold weather. Our climate is one of extremes: biting icy winds, sometimes of passionate strength, relentless stair-rod rain and, in winter, vast undulating snowscapes darkened here and there by the gaunt outlines of leafless trees and coppices. In the summer it is

HAILES ABBEY,
GLOUCESTERSHIRE

The ruins of one of the most important abbeys in England, built in the thirteenth century and dissolved in the reign of Henry VIII. It was stripped of its treasures, including the lead roof, and the building was demolished for its stone.

often warm and sultry and, apart from the occasional intrusion of low-flying aircraft, quiet, gentle and deceptively private.

As I write this sitting out in the warm April sun I can hear the cuckoo (who arrived last week) calling from the valley and I am reminded of Wordsworth:

> 'Oh blithe Newcomer! I have heard,
> I hear thee and rejoice.
> Oh Cuckoo! shall I call thee bird,
> Or but a wandering voice?'

It also reminds me of the first year we moved to the country and hearing the same sweet notes, I said to my town-bred chilren,

> 'Oh listen there's the cuckoo.'
> 'What's a cuckoo,' said my daughter.
> 'Oh don't be silly, Emily,' said my son.
> 'It's a male pheasant.'

The first swallows and house martins have just arrived this year and are flying high, feeding on the insects to build up their strength after their long, long flight from Africa. The garden is recovering from its winter battering in a host of different shades of green and the daffodils (late this year) herald the bosky floral days to come.

Truly this is a lovely part of the world. It has, of course, become increasingly popular in the last few years, not least because of the easy access from the two motorways, the M4 and the M5, a fact that has annoyed many of the locals except when it comes to selling their houses. Anyone trying to pass through Bibury on a summer day will understand what I mean; stone-wall-to-wall cars and hot-dog stalls. And then there is the attraction of the Royal triangle, as it is so called, that area of the Cotswolds so beloved of princes and princesses, which really does bring out the gawpers.

But on the whole there is enough room here to absorb the extra flow of people. Some of them, the weekenders, have done much to save many of the more derelict farm buildings and cottages, but at the same time they have tended to disrupt, with their noisy cars and their noisy parties, the social life of the somnolent villages. Everything has to change though. The area is doing so much to attract the tourist trade that things will never be the same again. For many people the image of the Cotswolds is best recorded in the pages of Laurie Lee's *Cider With Rosie*. For me it is my own lovely warm house on the valley side, surrounded by my family, my cats and dogs and my garden, the badgers, rabbits and foxes that saunter through our fields, and warm friendship of the village people who might, one day, accept me as one of them. For many though the Cotswolds will be engraved on their minds by this informative, beautifully put together and tellingly illustrated book, which taught me as much about this sainted area as anything I have ever read.

INTRODUCTION

On a midwinter day the sun hangs low in the pale-blue sky, grazing the wooded hillside and casting long shadows downwards to Broadway, that 'show piece' of Cotswold villages, lying at the foot of the steep escarpment known locally as Fish Hill. A biting wind gusts through the wide main street and up the slopes of the Edge, carrying with it fine particles of rain from the dark storm that approaches from the Malvern Hills, twenty-three miles to the west, sweeping across the Vale of Evesham. Rising from the level plain like an island in a sea of green, Bredon Hill is shrouded in cloud. On such occasions a local weather rhyme warns:

> 'When Bredon Hill puts on his hat
> Ye men of the Vale, beware of that.'

And looking across the plain where Shakespeare's Avon meanders lazily to the Severn, a heavy storm is clearly on its way.

More than any other scene, the view from Fish Hill, 800 feet above sea level, encapsulates much that is typically Cotswold. To the south-west the Edge, as it is commonly called, rises from the flat valleys of the Avon and the Severn. In the distance, ten miles away, can be discerned the highest point in the Cotswolds, Cleeve Hill, reaching 1,084 feet. The road from Broadway to Winchcombe leads towards it, running along the foot of the Edge. At intervals, tucked into the slopes, are several delightful villages, of which Stanway is the most famous, with its impressive seventeenth-century gatehouse. But Stanton, with its beautifully preserved golden-stone cottages set against the wooded backdrop of Shenberrow Hill, is a gem.

From the summit of the Edge Snowshill appears to the west, perched on the side of a minor escarpment, its houses clustered around the church. In winter the village is often cut off by snow. Here can be found a sixteenth-century manor house with a beautifully terraced garden, overlooking a steep valley that leads down from the wolds to Broadway.

Within this small area there are high hills, steep escarpments, rolling uplands, wooded coombs, swift-flowing streams, hill villages, small farmsteads, ancient sites, stately homes and lowly dwellings. But, more than anything else, it is the stone that gives the region its distinctive character and uniqueness.

Nowhere in Britain has the underlying rock had such a dominant effect on the landscape and architecture. There is stone in abundance, bringing beauty and harmony to every field, village and town. It lies close to the surface and when it is first removed from the ground it is easy to work, but it gradually hardens on exposure to the air until it is able to withstand centuries of weathering. It makes excellent building material and throughout the ages has been fashioned into an infinite variety of structures: from prehistoric burial mounds to magnificent churches; from humble cottages to great mansions; from dry-stone walls to castle ramparts.

In time the stone mellows to become a colour that is impossible to describe: ever-changing, shifting subtly from one moment to the next with each variation in the weather and the light. Buildings made from this mysterious stone, as J. B. Priestley said, 'knew the trick of keeping the lost sunlight of centuries glimmering about them'.

The stone is limestone, known as oolite, or eggstone, because of its structure of rounded granules that resemble the roe of fish. It was formed under enormous pressures millions of years ago from the powdered shells of primitive sea organisms. Cataclysmic changes in the earth's crust forced the sea bed upwards to create a belt of golden limestone that stretches from the coast of Dorset north-east to the coast of Yorkshire. But it is within a relatively small region that the limestone has prevailed, preventing the intrusion of uglier and cheaper building materials and bringing an unspoilt harmony to what has now been designated an Area of Outstanding Natural Beauty: the Cotswolds. There is disagreement about the precise limits of this unique area. For this book the limestone has been allowed to dictate the boundaries; it includes, therefore, only those villages and towns in which the stone predominates.

The most northerly point is Meon Hill, a few miles north of Chipping Campden. From here the Edge sweeps south-west for nearly forty miles to Dursley and then heads south for another twenty miles to Bath, 'the golden city'. Malmesbury is included by taking a north-easterly line from Bath to Cirencester. From Cirencester the boundary turns east to Fairford and Little Faringdon and then north to Burford. Resuming a north-easterly direction from Burford, there is a small detour at Chipping Norton to

BATH, AVON

The Roman *Aquae Sulis*, meaning 'the waters of Sulis', the Celtic goddess of the springs. Renowned for its warm natural spa waters, the city (seen here from Alexandra Park on Beechen Cliff) is situated at the southernmost tip of the limestone escarpment and rises up out of the Bristol Avon valley to adorn the steep slopes of the surrounding hills with a wealth of Georgian architecture built from the limestone.

include Great Tew and the Rollright Stones. Finally returning, by way of Moreton-in-Marsh, to Meon Hill.

The Cotswolds lie mainly in Gloucestershire, where the escarpment rises abruptly from the Severn valley to dip gently down into Oxfordshire. In the south the wolds extend into Avon and Wiltshire. While in the north they include a small corner of Warwickshire and an even tinier portion of Hereford and Worcester – namely Broadway.

Many clear streams and rivers rise in the high wolds, cleansed by the limestone. A few flow west into the Severn; the majority – like the Windrush, Churn, Leach and Coln – flow east into the Thames, which also has its source on the wolds. Their beginnings are far from spectacular, appearing more as puddles or trickles than gushing springs. But within a short distance, perhaps only a few hundred yards, the waters form into crystal-clear streams, sliding smoothly over the richly coloured limestone to follow the slope of the valleys down through idyllic villages and ancient towns.

The people who lived on the wolds in pre-Christian times believed that the life-giving waters were sacred, inhabited by powerful spirits who required worship and sacrificial offerings. Near the River Coln, high on the wooded hillside above the villa at Chedworth (where even the Romans had a water shrine) there is an ancient burial mound, or barrow. Such Stone Age relics can be found throughout the Cotswolds. Belas Knap, near Winchcombe, and Hetty Pegler's Tump, near Stroud, are fine examples of the 'long barrow' type of construction, built of stone and covered with earth.

The remains of Iron Age hill-forts stretch along the entire length of the Edge. Some – like Nottingham Hill, north-east of Cheltenham – extend for well over twenty acres, although there is little that can be seen today except grass-covered mounds and ditches. In prehistoric times the valleys were densely wooded and pitted with natural obstacles that made travelling difficult. Important lines of communication, therefore, evolved along the 'highways', the routes that kept mainly to the high ground and formed a network of tracks that criss-crossed the wolds, linking one settlement with another.

When the Romans invaded Britain in the first century AD they advanced rapidly into the Cotswolds and established major military roads like Fosse Way, Ermin Way and Akeman Street. Strategically placed at their intersection a new town grew up, expanding in size until, with the exception of London, it became the largest city in Britain: *Corinium*

Dobunnorum. It remained Roman, or Romano-British, until the Saxons captured the city in the sixth century and changed its name back to *Coryn Ceastre*, or Cirencester.

Apart from the limestone, nothing has shaped the Cotswolds more than wool. The very name itself is derived from the Anglo-Saxon *cote*, meaning a sheepfold, and *wold*, a tract of uncultivated upland. In the Middle Ages vast flocks of sheep, known as 'Cotswold Lions', were bred for their long wool. At first it was exported raw to Europe, but when it was manufactured into cloth it became such a major industry that it dominated the English economy for several centuries, making immense fortunes for the wool and cloth merchants. This wealth can be seen today in their splendid manors and fine houses but, more particularly, in the 'wool' churches they endowed, like Cirencester, Fairford, Northleach and Chipping Campden. Smaller and less ornate churches can be found in almost every village and hamlet. The majority are Norman, but there are a few, like Duntisbourne Rouse, with evidence of Saxon construction.

There were great abbeys at Malmesbury, Winchcombe, Cirencester and Hailes, attracting thousands of pilgrims each year in search of miraculous cures or the absolution of their sins. Many of these monastic institutions grew wealthy from the prosperity of the wool industry, owning much of the grazing land and even demolishing entire villages in order to create more. Great markets sprang up all over the Cotswolds and towns like Moreton-in-Marsh and Stow-on-the-Wold in the north and Minchinhampton and Tetbury in the south became important centres for the trading of wool.

Financially, the system was heavily biased in favour of the merchants. They bought the wool and distributed it to underpaid spinners and weavers who worked the fleece into cloth in their homes. The woven wool was then taken by the clothiers to their own fulling mills, where it was shrunk and thickened into cloth. Their mills, many of which were originally built to grind corn, were situated beside the streams and rivers that flowed down from the high wolds.

Fuller's earth, used in the clothmaking process, was found around Stroud and in consequence the area became the centre for the cloth industry, attracting craftsmen in their hundreds to the steep-sided valleys with fast-flowing streams that were ideal for powering water mills. By the beginning of the nineteenth century steam power, far more suitable for driving the heavy machinery necessary for mass production, had replaced water power and the bulk of cloth manufacture shifted to Yorkshire, bringing the 'golden age' of the Cotswolds to an end.

The consequences were disastrous. Families were faced with starvation. Many died. Others moved away in search of work. Poverty was rife. The population declined rapidly and the wolds were left to the sheep. Throughout the Industrial Revolution the region was left relatively untouched. It was this lack of development, with so many unspoilt villages and towns, that led to the birth of a new and lucrative industry – tourism.

The invasion of visitors from all over the world has to some extent ruined the atmosphere of villages like Bourton-on-the-Water or the Slaughters. But visit them out of season, or early on a summer's morning before the coaches arrive, and nowhere will you find a more charming and tranquil scene. Throughout the Cotswolds there are many villages, rarely visited, that are as attractive as the 'tourist traps'. There are narrow lanes that lead into secret valleys. There are sparkling, trout-filled streams that are seldom explored. And, for those who prefer solitude, there are always the high wind-swept wolds where you can stroll for mile after mile, gazing over the limestone countryside, with only the sheep and the larks for company.

CLEEVE HILL,
GLOUCESTERSHIRE

'Cleeve Cloud', at 1,084 feet, is the highest point in the Cotswolds. During the Iron Age the limestone cliff formed part of the defences of a large hill-fort, the ditches of which are now covered with grass.

CHIPPING CAMPDEN, BROADWAY AND THE NORTH-WESTERN EDGE

Built mainly of stone dug from local quarries, the towns and villages of the Cotswolds have an architectural style that is unique. This simplified Gothic style, known as the 'Cotswold vernacular', has dominated every building – whether a manor or a barn – for centuries. And despite Renaissance, Georgian and Victorian influences it has survived.

It was perfected after the Dissolution of the Monasteries, when the monastic masons were forced to find work in the towns and villages. They adapted the Elizabethan style of architecture, constructing manor houses, cottages, farms and barns on the same basic design. Essentially functional, the foundations are solid, with sturdy walls and steep-pitched roofs to carry the weight of the stone slates. The main features are dormers, gables, heavy square chimney stacks and small windows with mullions, transoms and drip mouldings.

Variations evolved within the basic formula, giving each building its own individuality. Yet despite differences in size, stature and embellishment each formed part of a harmonious whole, blending naturally into the limestone landscape from which the building material originally came.

Many of the old cottages were erected by the cottagers themselves, simply built and made to last. The walls are solid, nearly two feet thick and filled with rubble from ground to eaves. The roofs are steep, not only to support the weight of the porous stone slates, but to enable the rain to flow quickly away. The slates are pegged on their timber supports in graduated courses: the largest at the eaves, the smallest at the ridge. Each of the twenty-six sizes of slate has a particular name, like Short Bachelors, Long Bachelors, Middle Wivutts and Short Becks. The granular structure of the limestone encourages the growth of lichens and mosses on the surface and, once weathered to a dark grey, the roofs look very attractive.

The steep pitch of the roof does not allow space for windows on the upper floor under the eaves. This problem was solved by topping the walls with miniature gables, in which a window was fitted to form the dormer. As the stone slates are almost indestructible, it is the supporting timbers that are likely to decay first, producing the characteristic

CHIPPING CAMPDEN, GLOUCESTERSHIRE

The old market town of Chipping Campden, nestling in a hollow between hills, is dominated by the elegant pinnacled tower of the church of St James. In the Middle Ages it was one of the richest wool-trading centres in the Cotswolds and has been said to have 'the most beautiful village street in England'.

sagging roofs on old and neglected properties. The drip mouldings over the doors and windows are essential when building with porous stone; a small projection being enough to keep the rainwater from penetrating the walls below.

The houses and cottages were sited wherever there was a suitable plot of flat ground and, whether on a hill or in a valley, the position of each dwelling varies in relation to the next. Seldom, even on a straight road, are the houses exactly in line. In hill villages like Snowshill the buildings fit into the hillside wherever space allows, with manor house, cottages, church and inn all at different angles and on various levels.

Every building, from the humblest cottage to the finest mansion to the grandest church, is constructed from the same oolite limestone, giving them an affinity with each other and with the landscape – an affinity that is found nowhere else in England. This rare harmony is best exemplified in Chipping Campden, Broadway and the villages of the North-Western Edge. Chipping Campden is the main town in this area of high hills and secluded coombs, with its magnificent 'wool' church and wide market street, containing buildings that span at least five centuries. Meon Hill forms the northernmost tip of the Cotswolds, its summit overlooked by Ilmington Downs, on whose slopes lie Ilmington and Hidcote Bartrim, containing the beautiful gardens of Hidcote Manor. In the south are the hill towns of Blockley and Snowshill, with its treasure-filled manor. Along the foot of the Edge, between Chipping Campden and Stanway, is world-famous Broadway and the charming golden-stone villages of Buckland and Stanton.

FISH HILL,
HEREFORD AND WORCESTER

There is a legend that Fish Hill, near Broadway, got its name from the fossil of a fish which was discovered in the stone quarries near the summit. Certainly, the limestone here is rich in fossils, ranging from tiny shells to large ammonites. The steepness of the escarpment makes it impossible to farm and so the slopes have been left undisturbed for centuries – except for the grazing of sheep.

CHIPPING CAMPDEN,
GLOUCESTERSHIRE

Chipping Campden's prosperity as an important wool centre is not only reflected in its glorious 'wool' church, but in the town itself. Almost every house was built by wealthy and influential men. William Grevel, described on a brass in the church as 'the flower of the wool merchants of all England', built a splendid house in the High Street in 1380, where he lived until his death in 1401. He left a considerable sum of money to help rebuild the parish church of St James. Another benefactor, both to the town and the church, was Sir Baptist Hicks. In 1613 he erected a magnificent Jacobean mansion on land beside the church. It was burnt down during the Civil War and all that remains are the lodges and gateway. Opposite he built a beautifully proportioned terrace of almshouses, leading to the church. In 1627 he also built the Market Hall, now owned by the National Trust.

DOVER'S HILL,
GLOUCESTERSHIRE

On the hill above the market town of Chipping Campden the escarpment forms a natural amphitheatre with a panoramic view over the Vale of Evesham. Here in about 1612 Robert Dover, a retired attorney, founded the Cotswold 'Olympick' games. Athletes came from miles around to enter the competitions. One of the most popular events was shin-kicking, in which the contestants, wearing boots tipped with metal, held each other by the shoulders and attempted to kick their opponent's legs. The games came to an end in 1852 when gangs of hooligans from the industrial towns of the Midlands invaded the arena. They were revived in 1951 for the Festival of Britain and today occur on the first Friday after Whitsun, followed the next day by the Scuttlebrook Wake, originally a pagan festival held to celebrate the coming of spring. The land belongs to the National Trust.

WILLERSEY, WARWICKSHIRE

Willersey is one of four villages lying along the foot of the north-west escarpment between Broadway and Meon Hill. The main street is wide and flanked by long, grass verges, with stone-built houses and cottages, dating from about 1650, set well back from the road. The old barn house seen here is adjacent to the late-seventeenth-century Pool House, with its stone gate pillars, overlooking the village duck pond. The gabled Bell Inn is opposite, with the church at the end of a quiet cul-de-sac. It has a fifteenth-century tower, with pinnacles and gargoyles, while the little north porch is thirteenth-century.

ILMINGTON, WARWICKSHIRE

Ilmington is on the northernmost tip of the Cotswolds. It lies at the foot of Windmill Hill, on the eastern side of the high Ilmington Downs, overlooking the Oxfordshire Stour valley. The houses and cottages, some built of brick and others of stone, are spread along the slopes with a banked village green sited at a fork in the road. There is also a smaller green beside the Howard Arms. The church of St Mary is mainly Norman with a sixteenth-century porch. Inside, the carved oak furnishings, installed in the 1930s, are the work of Robert Thompson, master-craftsman of Kilburn in Yorkshire. Ilmington is an area rich in supernatural tales: from the appearance of a spectral 'Night Coach', driven by six ghostly horses and followed by a pack of phantom hounds, to the ghost of Edmund Golding, a parish clerk who died in 1793, which haunts the churchyard at midnight.

BROADWAY HILL, HEREFORD AND WORCESTER

The winter winds blow cold on the exposed summit of Broadway Hill, where everything freezes: the snow is polished into a glistening surface of ice and every branch and twig is sheathed in brittle glass. It is a scene that is in sharp contrast to the pleasant warmth and friendliness of early summer, with bubbling children and picnics on the grass. Yet, as they relax in the sun, how many are aware that in 1661 three people were hanged here for murder: a mother and her two sons, one of whom was left in chains to rot. It was a murder that none of them could have committed. For two years later the alleged murder victim returned, relating an incredible story of kidnapping, slavery in Turkey and eventual escape. The mystery was never adequately resolved and became known as the 'Campden Wonder'.

BROADWAY BEACON, HEREFORD AND WORCESTER

Broadway Hill, at 1,024 feet above sea level, is the second highest point in the Cotswolds, with magnificent views that extend over twelve counties. It was traditionally used as a beacon site on which a signal fire was lit to warn of an enemy's approach, or to transmit news quickly from one end of the country to the other. It is reputed that the wife of the sixth Earl of Coventry wanted to know whether the summit could be seen from Croome Court, the family seat near Worcester, some fifteen miles away. The Earl arranged for a bonfire to be lit on the hill and, realizing that it was visible, ordered a tower to be built on the spot. The folly was designed at the close of the eighteenth century by James Wyatt, who used a darker and moodier stone than that found locally.

LONGLAND'S FARM HILL, GLOUCESTERSHIRE

The influence of the Vale of Evesham, with its wide variety of market-garden produce, can be seen on the hillsides around Chipping Campden. In addition to fields of corn and Brussels sprouts, there are orchards, soft-fruit plantations and strawberry fields. But the influence of the wolds is strong too and sheep graze on any uncultivated patch of land. In winter it is common practice to leave the brussel sprout stalks for the sheep to eat. Since the mid-eighteenth century, the cross-breeding of sheep has developed breeds that are prolific and quickly produce meaty carcasses of lamb. The sheep here are 'mules', cross-bred from a Bluefaced Leicester ram and a hardy Scottish Blackface ewe.

WESTERN ESCARPMENT, HEREFORD AND WORCESTER

The roads that lead to Broadway Hill are part of an ancient 'high way' network that criss-crossed the wolds, enabling the traveller to avoid difficult ground. The ridgeway that runs along the Edge has been opened up to form the Cotswold Way. It is not strictly the resurrection of an ancient route, but more a linking together of existing rights of way. It was conceived in the 1950s by the local branch of the Ramblers' Association. The idea was shelved through lack of money and support until the late 1960s, when it was revived by Gloucestershire County Council. Today nearly 100 miles of footpath has been opened up to walkers. The Cotswold Way, keeping as far as possible to the Edge, stretches from Chipping Campden in the north to Bath in the south.

MIDDLE HILL,
HEREFORD AND WORCESTER

In the early fourteenth century the main road to Broadway came down from Middle Hill by way of Coneygree Lane to Bury End, the site of the original village. The ancient church of St Eadburgha is now a mile away from the present 'broad way', which abandoned the track up Middle Hill for the alternative route up Fish Hill. At Bury End is Abbots Grange, a fourteenth-century manor house with Elizabethan alterations. It was once the summer retreat of the Abbot of Evesham. By the end of the seventeenth century the new village had isolated the old, the ancient church was abandoned and another, St Michael's, was built nearer the village. St Eadburgha's has now, after years of neglect, been renovated. Sir Thomas Phillips, one of England's greatest book and manuscript collectors, is buried in the churchyard.

BROADWAY,
HEREFORD AND WORCESTER

From Fish Hill, with its spectacular views, the road winds some 600 feet down the escarpment in a series of wide curves to drop into the main street of Broadway. This village has been called the 'show piece' of the Cotswolds and certainly there are many who come to its broad, green-verged street to see its attractive rows of stone cottages, with their bow windows, dormers and perfectly graduated stone-tiled roofs. During the coaching era, the village had twenty-three inns, the most important being the White Hart. It was purchased in 1830 by General Lygon, who planted beech trees in the grounds of his estate above the village, setting out the formation of troops in the Battle of Waterloo. The inn was bought by his astute butler, who promptly renamed it the Lygon Arms and was allowed to use the family coat of arms on the sign.

HIDCOTE BARTRIM, GLOUCESTERSHIRE

Hidcote Bartrim, consisting of a few thatched stone cottages, a duck pond, a well and a farm, is in a secluded cul-de-sac beyond Hidcote Manor. Its main street, no wider than a narrow lane, ends in open fields which produce a variety of crops from strawberries to potatoes. Across the open countryside, less than a mile distant, lies the neighbouring and equally attractive hamlet of Hidcote Boyce, with its seventeenth-century manor, Hidcote House. Footpaths climb the hillside to Ilmington Downs, 854 feet above sea level, with views across the Vale of Moreton and the Vale of Evesham. Meon Hill appears almost below, with its Iron Age hill-fort silently guarding the northernmost tip of the Cotswolds.

HIDCOTE MANOR GARDEN, GLOUCESTERSHIRE

On the western slopes of Ilmington Downs, four miles north-east of Chipping Campden, was a wild, windswept uncultivated area of farmland, consisting of nearly 300 acres, a few specimen trees, a late-seventeenth-century manor house with its attendant thatched cottages and a lovely view over the Vale of Evesham. In 1907 it was acquired by Lawrence Waterbury Johnston, a soldier and farmer, who decided to make a garden. For seven years he laboured: planning, digging and planting to create what has now become one of the world's most famous gardens, Hidcote Manor Garden. Now owned by the National Trust, there are gardens here to suit all tastes: the White Garden, the Stilt Garden, the Old Garden, the Pillar Garden, the Terrace Garden with its gazebo, Mrs Winthrop's Garden with its pair of Hardy Chusan Palms, the Long Walk, the Bathing Pool Garden, the Stream Garden, and many more.

STANTON,
GLOUCESTERSHIRE

The road to Stanton, overhung by oak and chestnut trees, opens up to reveal an attractive, well-preserved, golden-stone village set against the dark backdrop of a tree-filled escarpment. John Wesley called it 'dear, delightful Stanton', and he spent many happy hours here in his youth, visiting friends. He attended the village church and preached from the timber pulpit – dated 1684. The carved ends of the medieval pews are gouged deep by ropes, where the shepherds tied their dogs. In the village the stone cottages and houses date from the beginning of the seventeenth century, a prosperous period for the Cotswold farmers and wool merchants. Less than 200 years later the village was falling into decay. It was saved by a wealthy architect from Lancashire, Philip Stott, later Sir Philip, who became the lord of the manor in 1906. He spent the next thirty years restoring the village.

BURHILL,
GLOUCESTERSHIRE

The Edge between Broadway and Cheltenham is so steep that very few minor roads manage the ascent. From Broadway to Stanway there are none and the villages of Buckland, Laverton and Stanton, lying in narrow wooded coombs tucked in under the escarpment, are reached by roads that lead nowhere else. Above Buckland and Laverton the Edge drops into a deep coomb, with the hill village of Snowshill at the head. Burhill forms a shoulder that slopes into the mouth of the coomb, through which a tiny stream flows north-westwards into the Vale of Evesham to join the Badsey Brook. The Cotswold Way, following an ancient track, climbs from Broadway up over the brow of the hill, where there are the remains of a prehistoric settlement, and continues along the wooded ridge towards Winchcombe and Cleeve Hill.

BLOCKLEY,
GLOUCESTERSHIRE

Blockley seems to belong more to the industrialized Stroud valleys than to the sheep-rearing villages of the northern wolds. Yet it has its origins firmly in wool. The parish was owned by the bishops of Worcester in medieval times and used as pastureland to graze their flocks. By the late eighteenth century, with the decline in the wool trade, Blockley had become industrialized. In 1823 no fewer than six mills were preparing silk for the ribbon-making factories of Coventry. In 1860 the levy on imported silk was removed, allowing foreign competition into the country and Blockley's industry went into decline. Today most of the mills have been converted into attractive cottages with the stream (which flows north-easterly to feed into the Knee Brook and then the Stour) running through their gardens. The village is built on a steep hillside with narrow, precipitous lanes dropping directly into the deep valley.

STANWAY,
GLOUCESTERSHIRE

Coscombe Quarry, on the top of the Cotswold escarpment above Stanway, produces Yellow Guiting stone, which mellows into a rich golden colour. Stanway House, at the foot of the ancient 'Stane', or 'Stone Way', is built of this glorious stone. The ornate seventeenth-century gatehouse is probably the work of the master-mason Timothy Strong of Little Barrington. It bears the arms of the Tracy family, who acquired the manor at the Dissolution from Tewkesbury Abbey. The manor house is Jacobean and stands in lovely gardens, surrounded by sloping parkland where sheep graze under ancient oaks. The church was built in the fourteenth century, but was heavily restored at the end of the nineteenth century.

BUCKLAND,
GLOUCESTERSHIRE

Buckland is about two miles
south-west of Broadway,
nestling in a secluded hollow at
the foot of Burhill. It is thought
to have the oldest rectory in
England, with an impressive
timbered hall that dates from the
fifteenth century. Buckland
Rectory was built by a former
rector, William Grafton, and
one of its windows contains the
badge of Edward IV. Mrs
Delany, letter writer and diarist,
lived in the village before her
marriage to Alexander
Pendarves in 1717. John Wesley
preached in the church of St
Michael, the east window of
which contains some splendid
fifteenth-century glass, judged
by some to be the finest in the
Cotswolds, and reputed to have
come from Hailes Abbey at the
Dissolution. It so impressed
William Morris, when he came
to Buckland towards the end of
the nineteenth century, that he
paid to have it releaded himself.

SNOWSHILL,
GLOUCESTERSHIRE

The road south from Broadway
to Snowshill, some two miles
distant, passes Bury End to hug
the eastern slopes of a deep
coomb, becoming steeper and
steeper as it approaches the high
wolds beyond Oat Hill.
Amazingly, the old Oxford to
Worcester road did not take this
route, ascending instead from
Bury End up the twisting
Coneygree Lane to Dor Knap
and Middle Hill, before passing
to the south of Snowshill. It fell
into disuse in the early sixteenth
century. The headwaters of the
Badsey Brook rise in this
coomb, where the woodlands
give way to rough pastureland,
suitable only for sheep, with
isolated farmsteads scattered on
the steep slopes. Above, a long
wooded crest marks the top of
the Edge, which drops abruptly
to the villages of Buckland,
Laverton and Stanton beyond.
In the winter the roads are often
impassable, with snow blowing
down from the open wolds to
create deep drifts that effectively
cut off the villages and
farmsteads.

SNOWSHILL, GLOUCESTERSHIRE

Snowshill in addition to being one of the most unspoilt of Cotswold villages is also one of the most remote. Built on the edge of a minor escarpment, just below Oat Hill, there is no room for further expansion. The land once belonged to the King of Mercia, who gave it to Winchcombe Abbey, whose property it remained until the Dissolution. It was one of a number of upland manors, like Charlton Abbots, Hawley and Roel, where the Abbey's huge flocks were allowed to graze before being driven down into the valleys to be washed and sheared. Snowshill Manor house now belongs to the National Trust and contains the incredible collection of bygones accumulated by Charles Wade.

SNOWSHILL, GLOUCESTERSHIRE

The village of Snowshill clusters around a triangular dry-stone-walled green in the middle of which stands a squat church. The old stone cottages are set at different angles and levels, fitting into the hillside wherever space allows. There is no single main street, but a number of interconnected roads that wind steeply up on to the wolds or down into the valley. The Norman church was completely rebuilt in 1864 and all that remains of the old building is a fifteenth-century font and a Jacobean pulpit. Nearby, in a group of Bronze Age burial mounds the skeleton of a warrior was found, together with a stone battle-axe and a bronze dagger, spear and pin. The discovery confirms the existence of a settlement on this site for thousands of years.

SNOWSHILL MANOR, GLOUCESTERSHIRE

The Manor of Snowshill dates from about 1500. It was altered in the seventeenth and eighteenth centuries and restored in the 1920s by the then owner, Charles Paget Wade. He was a human magpie, devoting his wealth to amassing a collection of strange and unusual objects. His family arms, in the entrance hall, bear the motto, *Nequid pereat* ('Let nothing perish'). Indeed, the curios of the past are packed into every room: toys, musical instruments, weaving and spinning tools, clocks, Tibetan scrolls, models of ships, Japanese armour and Persian lamps. The 'Great Garret' is known as 'The Room of a Hundred Wheels', where wheels of every sort can be discovered from penny-farthing bicycles to model farm wagons – and numbering far more than a hundred. Wade gave the entire collection to the National Trust in 1951, five years before his death, together with the manor house and its beautiful terraced garden.

SNOWSHILL WOLD, GLOUCESTERSHIRE

The wolds above Snowshill rise to over 900 feet above sea level and have been turned into arable land that is planted with winter sprouts and summer corn. The countryside is open and windswept, with large fields separated by dry-stone walls, where wild flowers thrive and hares are plentiful. The dry-stone walling has become a feature of the Cotswold fields; although it is a comparatively recent addition, due to the Enclosure Acts of the seventeenth and eighteenth centuries. The stone weathers to an antique grey and is quickly covered with lichen and wayside plants.

STOW-ON-THE-WOLD AND THE NORTH-EASTERN WOLDS

If the Cotswold limestone provided a readily available and inexaustible supply of building material, wool provided the wealth to create some of the grandest houses, mansions and churches in the country.

The wolds have supported sheep since prehistoric times and one of the oldest crafts is the weaving of wool into cloth: not only for domestic use, but also for barter and trade. There is evidence that the Dobunni – an ancient British tribe whose fortified capital was at Bagendon, near Cirencester – exported woollen cloaks to Rome in the third century. The Romans encouraged the trade, setting up 'imperial weaving manufactories', where, according to the geographer Dionysius Peregetes, the wool was spun so fine that it resembled a 'spider's web'. There was probably a 'weaving manufactory' at Cirencester, the Roman capital of *Corinium Dobunnorum*. The town's Corinium Museum contains an impressive collection of Roman remains, including many everyday objects that are connected with spinning and weaving.

After the Roman legions had been recalled to Rome, the Saxon invaders continued the trade in wool as the names of many hills, fields and villages testify: the Shiptons (Shipton, Shipton Solers and Shipton Oliffe) mean 'sheep farmstead'; Sheepscombe, 'sheep's valley'; Yanworth, 'lamb enclosure'; Sherborne, the 'clear waters' where the sheep were washed. At Salmonsbury, near Bourton-on-the-Water, the excavation of a Saxon weaver's hut unearthed the remains of an upright loom.

Long before the Norman Conquest wool was being exported to Europe, where the Flemish and Italian weavers produced cloth of excellent quality from the raw fleeces – claiming that the finest wool in Europe was British and the finest wool in Britain was Cotswold.

England's virtual monopoly of the wool trade during the Middle Ages was due to two factors: the extermination of the wolf, which flourished on the Continent, and the fact that the island enjoyed relative peace, while Europe was the battleground for one war after another. It was extremely difficult to rear sheep in large numbers in such a hostile environment and the Europeans were forced to import their wool from England.

THE REDLANDS, OXFORDSHIRE

To the north-east of Chipping Norton are the 'Redlands', named after the reddish-brown colour of the soil, which is rich and fertile because of the presence of iron. It is one of the best corn-producing regions in England, with wheat, barley and oats being the most common crop. After the grain has been harvested, the farmer generally sets light to the stubble in order to clear the ground of weeds in readiness for the next crop.

Between the twelfth and fifteenth centuries the English economy was dominated by the export of wool. Most of the Cotswolds was owned by Norman knights, rewarded with land for their part in the Conquest, and the great abbeys, who increased their wealth by turning more and more of the wolds into rough pasture. In many instances entire villages were destroyed to enable the huge flocks to graze freely. By the beginning of the thirteenth century there were four times as many sheep as people.

Edward II, sensing that there were even greater profits to be made by producing cloth in England, encouraged communities of Flemish weavers to settle in the country. This proved to be a success and the export of wool declined. By the sixteenth century the merchants of the Cotswolds had made immense fortunes from the wool and cloth industry, using their wealth to build fine houses and mansions for themselves and to rebuild the old churches in magnificent Perpendicular style. As one of them said: 'I praise God and ever shall. It is the sheep hath paid for it all.'

Stow-on-the-Wold became famous, not so much as a wool town but as a major sheep market. Early in the eighteenth century, Daniel Defoe recorded that, on one day alone, over 20,000 sheep were sold in its market place. The largest town in the North-Eastern Wolds is Moreton-in-Marsh, another wool market town, with its Market Hall and wide main street. Within this area is the Jacobean mansion of a wealthy wool merchant, Chastleton House, and some of the most delightful villages in the Cotswolds: the Tews, the Swells and the Slaughters.

WYCK RISSINGTON, GLOUCESTERSHIRE

Three Rissington villages lie about a mile apart on the eastern side of the Dikler and Windrush valleys. The most northerly is Wyck Rissington, a small, well-kept stone village with a wide green, a duck pond and a church in which the composer Gustav Holst was once organist. In the churchyard of St Laurence is a nine-foot-high yew tree, which has been clipped to form a living cross.

LOWER SWELL,
GLOUCESTERSHIRE

Working with metal is one of the oldest of Cotswold crafts. Until comparatively recently the blacksmith was the most important craftsman in the rural community. Without his skill with metal all the other craftsmen would have had no tools with which to carry on their trade. He also produced weapons, armour, ploughshares, fittings for wagons and tackle for horses; he repaired the scythes that cut the corn, the shears that clipped the wool and the chisels that shaped the stone; he was expected to adapt old bits of metal from a machine or tool to restore another one. Anything made of metal was potentially useful and the walls of his forge would be hung with all kinds of odds and ends. Once he was revered with awe: a mysterious, devil-like figure who was master of fire. Today, the blacksmith has lost his power. His is a dying craft and, in the northern Cotswolds, the Old Smithy in Lower Swell is the last to survive.

UPPER SWELL,
GLOUCESTERSHIRE

'Swell', it is believed, is derived from a shortening of 'Our Lady's Well', which still exists in Lower Swell. There is a legend that an ancient standing stone, the Whittlestone, used to come down from the wolds to drink at the well on the stroke of midnight. It was moved about a century ago and now stands in the grounds of the vicarage. There is a nineteenth-century mill at Upper Swell, its great mill-wheel fed by a large pond. The village itself is grouped around the manor house and church. There are an unusually high number of prehistoric barrows in this area. David Royce, rector of Lower Swell and an archaeologist, gathered together a considerable collection of flints, arrowheads and Roman pottery found locally.

LOWER SLAUGHTER, GLOUCESTERSHIRE

Lower Slaughter is less than a mile downstream from Upper Slaughter. At the head of the village, there is a nineteenth-century corn mill, complete with its tall chimney and water-wheel. The Slaughter Brook running beside the mill is broad and shallow. It is curious that the mill should be built of red brick, given that the neighbourhood is noted for its quarries, which in the Middle Ages supplied high-quality stone for the building of many Oxford colleges. Some have been worked until only recently and the quarry at Eyford Hill is still producing slates. Valentine Strong, one of the family of master masons from Little Barrington, built the manor house in about 1640.

LOWER SLAUGHTER, GLOUCESTERSHIRE

The Slaughter Brook flows from the old mill through the centre of the village, passing under little stone footbridges to a tree-shaded green opposite the church and old manor house. Hidden discreetly up the manor's driveway is a sixteenth-century dovecote, considered to be one of the finest in Gloucestershire. In the centre of this neat and lawn-trimmed village is a group of simple, beautifully proportioned cottages, all built of traditional stone and blending perfectly with one another. It is the brook though that makes the village so attractive. Contained by limestone banks, the shallow trout-filled water is clear and sparkling, running over a bed of stone and gravel. Nearby a gaggle of pure white geese paddle between the bridges. The Eye joins the Dikler near Bourton-on-the-Water and within a mile they feed into the Windrush.

MORETON-IN-MARSH, GLOUCESTERSHIRE

Where the Fosse Way crosses the Great Road of Worcester it becomes the wide main street of Moreton-in-Marsh, linking the town directly with Stow-on-the-Wold, Northleach and Cirencester. The Romans had a camp here when the road was built in the first century AD. It has been a market town since the thirteenth century when the lord of the manor, the Abbot of Westminster, was granted a charter to hold a weekly market. The Tudor-style Market Hall, built in 1887, is now the Town Hall. The source of the Evenlode is in nearby Batsford Park, to the north-west. At Moreton-in-Marsh the river caused considerable flooding until the road was raised. It is thought that the town's original name of 'Moreton Henmarsh' came from the fact that the low-lying land was marshy and much frequented by moorhens.

DONNINGTON, GLOUCESTERSHIRE

The Dikler rises on Bourton Down, a few miles north-west of Bourton-on-the-Hill, flows down a wooded gulley and disappears underground. It re-emerges in the lake at Donnington Brewery, where the river has been dammed to drive a large water-wheel. There has been a corn mill here since the early fourteenth century and, in 1865, the Arkell family turned it into a brewery. It laid claim to being the smallest brewery in England until the newer and smaller Cellar Brewery in Cirencester was established. Donnington grows its own barley and, with Worcester hops and power from its water-wheel, it supplies seventeen public houses with traditional Cotswold ale. The village of Donnington, two miles east, is famous as the place where Lord Astley and his army surrendered to the Parliamentarians in 1646.

STOW-ON-THE-WOLD, GLOUCESTERSHIRE

'Stow-on-the-Wold, where the wind blows cold' is an old rhyme that refers to this hilltop town's exposed position. At 800 feet above sea level it is the highest town in the Cotswolds and is situated between the valleys of the Dikler and Evenlode at the intersection of eight roads, the most important being the Roman Fosse Way leading across the wolds to Cirencester. It developed into a major market town. The spacious market square, surrounded by some fine old gabled houses, is positioned away from the busy highway. The traditional market cross portrays Henry I granting the Abbot of Evesham the right to hold a weekly market at Stow St Edwards, or Edwardstowe, as Stow was known in the twelfth century. The King's Arms, shown here, was built in the early sixteenth century and became a major staging post for coach traffic on the route between London and Worcester.

DIKLER VALLEY, GLOUCESTERSHIRE

Stow-on-the-Wold is situated on a high ridge, where it is exposed to the unchecked winds that blow across the wolds to and from Cleeve Hill. In the eighteenth century it was said, jokingly, that the town lacked earth, fire and water, but had plenty of air. However the valleys that surround the town are lush and green with an abundance of natural springs and water. The limestone is porous, retaining moisture even in dry weather, a factor that keeps the pastures green and makes the Cotswolds good sheep-grazing land. The view from the Fosse Way, on the western edge of the town, slopes steeply into the Dikler valley and less than a mile away, hidden in the fold of the wooded hills, are Upper and Lower Swell.

GREAT TEW, OXFORDSHIRE

The cottages in Great Tew and Little Tew are built of ironstone in the traditional Cotswold style, with mullioned windows, drip mouldings and moulded doorframes. Some are thatched, while others are roofed with stone tiles. The Norman church at Great Tew contains a memorial to Lucius Cary, Lord Falkland, who was killed at the Battle of Newbury in 1643 fighting for Charles I. The Falkland Arms beside the village green was named after him. Lord Falkland's Elizabethan house was destroyed by fire and a new manor was built in the nineteenth century by Matthew Robinson Boulton, the son of Matthew Boulton of Birmingham, considered by some to be the 'Father of the Industrial Revolution'. The estate was owned by Colonel Stratton at the beginning of the nineteenth century and was managed by John Claudius Loudon, a Scottish architect and agriculturalist. Much of the village's present attractiveness is due to Loudon's landscaping skills.

BOURTON-ON-THE-WATER, GLOUCESTERSHIRE

Buckle Street, or Buggildway, meets the Fosse Way where it crosses the River Windrush. Here the Romans built a bridge to carry the road over the swift-flowing river and nearby, at Salmonsbury, there is evidence of an Iron Age hill-fort, where a considerable number of iron currency bars have been unearthed. It was on the edge of this ancient settlement that Bourton-on-the-Water sprang up, its graceful low stone bridges spanning the Windrush at intervals, creating such a delightful scene that it has been alluded to as 'the Venice of the Cotswolds'. The Norman church, built on Saxon foundations, was largely demolished in 1784 and rebuilt with a domed tower, a feature that is unique in the Cotswolds.

EVENLODE,
GLOUCESTERSHIRE

Although many Cotswold villages include rivers in their names, only two bear their exact name: Windrush and Evenlode. Both rivers are tributaries of the Thames. The Evenlode rises to the north-west of Moreton-in-Marsh, flowing south-eastwards through a string of delightful low-lying villages, the first of which is Evenlode. This charming village, spread in the broad, lush and wooded valley beside the sparkling stream, is built of Cotswold stone. There are stone-tiled cottages and farmhouses, an early-nineteenth-century rectory and a medieval church. The church of St Edward contains a carved fifteenth-century oak pulpit in the shape of a wineglass. The chancel arch is late Norman and there are several interesting eighteenth- and nineteenth-century tombs in the churchyard.

UPPER SLAUGHTER,
GLOUCESTERSHIRE

The tiny River Eye, a tributary of the Dikler and Windrush, rises in the wolds above Eyford Park and flows through the timeless villages of Upper and Lower Slaughter, where it is known as Slaughter Brook. There are a number of explanations for the unusual name of Slaughter. Some say that it is derived from the Old English *slohtre*, meaning a slough or muddy place. While others maintain that it refers to the abundance of sloe trees, or blackthorns, in the locality. Upper Slaughter is situated on the hillside above the stream, with a few farm buildings and cottages on the other side. These are linked by a number of stone footbridges and a ford.

CHASTLETON, OXFORDSHIRE

Chastleton House was built in 1603 by Walter Jones, a wealthy Cotswold wool merchant, who bought the estate from Robert Catesby, one of the conspirators of the Gunpowder Plot to blow up Parliament and James I. It is a superb, perfectly symmetrical, five-gabled Jacobean manor house with two towers that has remained virtually unaltered since it was built. The interior still contains much of its original furniture and one of the house's many treasures is the Bible that Charles I carried to his execution in 1649. The grounds contain a rare topiary garden laid out in the seventeenth century. In the field opposite is a charming dovecote built on arches, dating from 1751. The church of St Mary the Virgin is mostly Norman. On the hilltop above Chastleton are the remains of an Iron Age hill-fort.

CHIPPING NORTON, OXFORDSHIRE

Chipping Norton is the highest town in Oxfordshire, situated on the western slopes of a hillside that was once the site of a Norman castle. 'Chipping' is derived from *ceapen*, an Old English word meaning market. There has been a market here since the thirteenth century. It was a major wool-trading town in the fifteenth century; the great 'wool' church of St Mary, built in Perpendicular style, testifys to its prosperity. Nearby, in Church Street, are the Henry Cornishe Almshouses, erected in 1640, an attractive row of gabled buildings of Cotswold stone. The main streets are wide and contain some fine eighteenth-century buildings. The Market Hall was built in 1842 and the Blue Boar has been an inn for at least 500 years. Here and there, stone archways offer glimpses of the past with narrow lanes running between the tiny terraced houses of the old cloth-weavers.

ROLLRIGHT STONES, OXFORDSHIRE

The Rollright Stones stand on an exposed ridge, 700 feet above sea level, a few miles north of Chipping Norton. They consist of a stone circle, a nearby eight-foot-high standing stone and, a quarter of a mile away, five stones that were probably part of a burial chamber. Bronze Age people arranged the irregular, unworked stones in a great 100-foot stone circle, known locally as the King's Men. There is a legend that they were an army that had been turned into stone by a witch. The solitary stone, known as the King's Stone, is said to be the king and the five standing stones are the Whispering Knights. The stone circle, although far less impressive than Stonehenge and Avebury, ranks next in importance and has been dated to between 1500 and 2000 BC. The stones vary in height from a few inches to seven feet.

CONDICOTE WOLD, GLOUCESTERSHIRE

Condicote is probably one of the oldest villages in the Cotswolds, standing bestride an ancient trackway, later improved by the Romans, known as Ryknield Street or Condicote Lane. This isolated village stands on a high ridge above and to the west of Donnington Brewery, close to the site of a Neolithic 'henge', a huge circular earthwork used for rituals. An extraordinary number of burial mounds and barrows surround the earthwork. The village is grouped around a walled green with an ancient wayside cross at the western end. There is a well and a spring. The little church is Norman, although restored in the nineteenth century. Condicote is a small farming community and, as the name suggests, it has long been associated with sheep.

CHELTENHAM, CIRENCESTER AND THE CENTRAL WOLDS

There is no shortage of building material in the Cotswolds. The oolite limestone, either exposed or lying just below the surface of the ground, provides a natural and inexhaustible supply of stones and slates. The Cotswolds is in effect a vast quarry, where every village once had its own communal pit or mine. Throughout the region the turf-covered depressions of abandoned workings fit perfectly into the landscape.

The soil is extremely shallow and when ploughed the limestone literally crumbles out of the ground. The stone used for erecting dry-stone walls is found a few feet down. It is dug on the site, at the edge of the field, and laid in courses, which are kept dry by 'combers', stones placed vertically on the top. The oolite, used in the construction of all manner of buildings from churches to barns, is found even deeper. When freshly quarried this fine-grained 'freestone' is soft and carved or sawn very easily, hardening with exposure to withstand centuries of weathering and wear.

When first removed from the ground it is pale, varying in colour from district to district depending on the amount of mineral iron present in the limestone. In the north, at Chipping Campden and Broadway, it is a deep golden colour. Around Painswick it is silver-grey. Towards the Oxfordshire border and the Tews it weathers to a deep orange-buff. In the Bath area to the south it is honey-gold. But even then the colours shift throughout the day, reflecting the play of light upon the surface of the stone and responding to the ever-changing moods of the English weather.

The Edge, where the limestone is exposed, is pockmarked with quarries. The quarry on Leckhampton Hill, above Cheltenham, not only supplied all the 'freestone' for the building of the Georgian spa town, but also the building material for miles around. 'Freestone' is the quarryman's name for fine-granuled, shell-free stone that can be carved deeply and sawn into smooth-surfaced blocks, called 'ashlar'.

The finest examples of the mason's skill with stone can be found in the magnificent Perpendicular 'wool' churches of Cirencester, Chipping Campden, Northleach and Fairford. The stone for St Paul's Cathedral in London and many of Oxford's colleges came from the Cotswold quarries.

COLESBOURNE PARK, GLOUCESTERSHIRE

The Hilcot Brook comes down from the high wolds, flowing through copper beech woods and open, rich-red farmland to Colesbourne Park, where it forms a lake before emptying into the River Churn. The park contains many rare trees planted by Squire Henry Elwes (1846-1922), who was co-author of the seven-volume classic work on *The Trees of Great Britain and Ireland*, published in 1913.

Stone roofing slates are dug from quarries where the limestone has been laid down in fissile layers, like those at Naunton. The roughly hewn stone blocks, when exposed to the frost, split easily into thin slates, which are then shaped and given peg-holes. They have been used since Roman times and provide excellent roofing material, weathering to a dark grey that is soon covered with moss and lichen.

The Central Wolds between Cheltenham and Cirencester contain many examples of the use of stone, dating back to prehistoric times. The long barrow at Belas Knap, above Winchcombe, proves that for over 4,000 years the method of dry-stone walling has hardly changed. The Romans built a grand villa near Chedworth with baths, servants' quarters, latrines, kitchens, bedrooms and a dining room with under-floor heating. Many Cotswold churches have Saxon origins, like St Michael's at Duntisbourne Rouse. The church of St John in the remote hill village of Elkstone is considered to be the best preserved Norman church in Gloucestershire. Monasteries like Hailes Abbey, built in the thirteenth century, turned large areas of the wolds into sheep-grazing land, growing extremely wealthy from the prosperous wool trade. The abbey was demolished at the Dissolution by Sir Thomas Seymour who used the stone to rebuild Sudeley Castle, one of the few surviving castles in the Cotswolds.

All roads lead to Cirencester, the 'capital' of the Cotswolds, including the Roman Fosse Way, Akeman Street and Ermin Way. The town contains many fine buildings, dating back to medieval times, with the eighteenth-century stone mansion of the Bathurst family standing on the edge of a fine park nearby.

DUNTISBOURNE LEER, GLOUCESTERSHIRE

Half-a-mile south-east of Duntisbourne Abbots is the tiny hamlet of Duntisbourne Leer, where the Dun Brook flows through a clear, shallow ford that almost laps the doorsteps of the farm and cottages. The hamlet belonged to the Abbey of Lire in France and the manor's former ownership is remembered by a fleur-de-lys carved on the chimney and doorhead of a farmhouse.

LECKHAMPTON HILL,
GLOUCESTERSHIRE

The limestone used for the building of Georgian Cheltenham came from the quarry on Leckhampton Hill, two miles south of the town. At the end of the eighteenth century Charles Brandon Trye of Leckhampton Manor constructed a primitive gravity-inclined railway to transport the stone from the quarry, beneath the edge of the high escarpment, down into the vale. Quarrying the hill was a thriving industry from Victorian times when horse-drawn trams and later engine-drawn trucks were used. Although the quarry is now abandoned, the quarrymen left behind a landmark that is said to rise straight from Hell, the Devil's Chimney. There is a legend that the Devil is trapped deep inside the rock below. In danger of collapse because of erosion, or for fear of setting him free, the column was strengthened with iron rods and mortar in 1985.

CHELTENHAM,
GLOUCESTERSHIRE

In 1716 a Cheltenham farmer, William Mason, noticed that flocks of pigeons gathered regularly in one of his fields to feed. He discovered they were pecking at crystals of salt deposited by a nearby spring. Finding that the spring was pure mineral water he sold the water in bottles. In 1740 his son-in-law, Captain Henry Skillicorne, built a brick edifice over the spring, installed a pump and called it a spa. It became fashionable for the physicians of the period to prescribe the 'taking of the medicinal waters' for all kinds of ailments. When George III came to Cheltenham in 1788 the spa received the royal seal of approval. It was not until 1816, however, when the Duke of Wellington was relieved of a liver disorder that large-scale development took place. A new town was designed on classical lines by brilliant architects, with wide tree-lined streets and open spaces.

WINCHCOMBE, GLOUCESTERSHIRE

Situated along a slope at the base of Langley Hill, in a winding coomb that drops down to the Vale of Evesham, Winchcombe blends naturally into its magnificent surroundings. The River Isbourne springs from high up on the escarpment, running along the length of the town and then north across the vale to join the Avon at Evesham. It is recorded that by the end of the twelfth century this tiny stream was driving at least two fulling mills for Winchcombe Abbey, one of the largest landowners in the Cotswolds. When the great abbey was completely demolished at the Dissolution, much of its stone went into the building of the town and nearby Sudeley Castle.

HAILES ABBEY, GLOUCESTERSHIRE

Hailes Abbey was founded in 1246 by Richard, Earl of Cornwall, King of the Romans and brother of Henry III. It was built to fulfil a vow that he had made four years earlier, when he was in danger of being shipwrecked off the Scilly Isles. He landed safely and gave thanks by sparing no cost in the erection of a magnificent abbey, sited below the Cotswold Edge, about three miles north-east of Winchcombe. For 300 years it grew in wealth and power until, in 1539, the abbey and its priceless treasures were surrendered to the Crown. The abbey became the property of Sir Thomas Seymour, who had it demolished. The ruins, with seventeen cloister arches, now belong to the National Trust and are managed by English Heritage.

WINCHCOMBE,
GLOUCESTERSHIRE

Winchcombe was once the seat of the Saxon kings of Mercia and capital of a separate shire, Winchcombeshire. In the late eighth century, King Offa built a nunnery here and his successor, Kenelf, founded an abbey that was soon dedicated to his martyred son, St Kenelm. The young prince had been murdered and his body hidden in a thicket. By a curious miracle the Pope in Rome received a note, carried by a dove from heaven, giving an exact account of the boy's death and the whereabouts of his body. The monks were guided by a white cow and a heavenly ray of light to the spot and the body was enshrined in the abbey at Winchcombe. The account of the young prince's martyrdom brought pilgrims from far and wide to visit the shrine and the abbey became rich and powerful. It was completely demolished at the Dissolution. Yet, strangely, the church of St Peter survived.

WINCHCOMBE,
GLOUCESTERSHIRE

Vineyard Street, lined with small porched cottages and pollarded limes, leads steeply down to the River Isbourne, where once the town's gossips were ducked. Beyond the stream the road climbs to the entrance gates of Sudeley Castle. If the name of the street suggests that vines were once grown on the sheltered south-facing slopes of the town, 'Tobacco Close' serves as a reminder that tobacco was also cultivated here. With the decline in the wool trade, the landowners of Winchcombe turned to growing tobacco. For fifty years the trade flourished. Queen Elizabeth I and James I both attempted, and failed, to stop the cultivation of the weed because it was against the interests of the West Indian tobacco merchants. Eventually, Parliament prevailed and early in the seventeenth century the planting of tobacco at Winchcombe ceased.

WINCHCOMBE, GLOUCESTERSHIRE

The great 'wool' church of St Peter was a joint venture between the Abbot of Winchcombe, who built the chancel, and Sir Ralph Boteler, who built the nave. It is remarkable for the fact that it was designed and completed in one architectural period – the late Perpendicular. It is not famed, however, for its fifteenth-century construction, but for the forty gargoyles, some gruesome and others comic, that decorate the exterior. Many have been given names like the 'Mad Hatter' and 'Kaiser Bill'. In addition to the church, Winchcombe contains a number of ancient inns – including the George Hotel, the Old Corner Cupboard Inn and the White Lion – many fine houses, some Tudor buildings and a row of attractive almshouses.

WINCHCOMBE WOLD, GLOUCESTERSHIRE

Beech woods are characteristic of the Cotswolds, generally surviving on the escarpment where the slopes are thick with trees or in areas that are difficult to plough, where they may be mixed with chestnut, larch and sycamore. The hedges are mainly hawthorn with dogwood and viburnum, the wayfarer's tree, supporting briar roses or traveller's joy. They provide cover for all kinds of wildlife from foxes and badgers to the tiniest shrew. The fields of reddish soil are sown with wheat and barley, and pheasants, partridges and hares blend into the landscape. The high wolds swell and dip, with hidden springs and wooded copses tucked into the folds. There are few features that are striking; instead, the landscape is gentle, open to the sky, allowing the ever-changing light to create an infinite variety of moods.

DUNTISBOURNE ROUSE, GLOUCESTERSHIRE

Duntisbourne Rouse is a tiny hamlet consisting of a few farm cottages in a deep, green hollow, near a ford across the Dun Brook. The church of St Michael is one of the smallest in the Cotswolds. It is perched on a high rise above the stream. At the east end, built into the steep slope, is a vaulted stone crypt under the chancel – an extremely rare feature in so small a building. It is a beautifully simple church, with Saxon origins and Norman alterations, that avoided the restorers and the wealthy wool merchants. The exterior walls are built of huge stones and the interior has areas of Saxon herringbone masonry. The misericord stalls, with carved vine leaves and grotesque heads, are believed to have come originally from Cirencester Abbey. In the churchyard there is a fourteenth-century cross with a long shaft.

DUNTISBOURNE ABBOTS, GLOUCESTERSHIRE

The Duntisbournes take the first part of their names from the Dun Brook that meanders south-east down the valley to enter the Churn at Cirencester. Duntisbourne Abbots is the largest of the four villages. It is built in terraces down the side of the valley around a small, sloping green. Below is a spring that once supplied the villagers' water. Before emptying into the brook, the spring pours into a large stone trough, where water plants flourish. The road becomes part of the brook, running between high walls and raised pavements. Here the carters used to wash their horses' hooves and clean the wheels of their carts. It is the only surviving water lane in the Cotswolds. The Norman church of St Peter is situated on a high bank in the centre of the village and has a Norman font. It was restored in 1872.

SUDELEY CASTLE, GLOUCESTERSHIRE

Sudeley Castle nestles in the 'fat' valley, as the Romans called the Winchcombe region some 1,600 years ago, because of the rich tributes of corn and wool they received from the area. Salt was also an essential commodity, used as a meat preservative when animals had to be slaughtered in the autumn because there wasn't enough fodder to feed them through the winter. High above Sudeley Castle there is evidence of one of the ancient 'salt ways' that ran from Droitwich to the Thames at Lechlade. The Romans worked salt deposits around Droitwich (*Salinae*), where the springs are said to be ten times saltier than ordinary sea water. The salt was loaded on to pack horses and transported throughout England.

SUDELEY CASTLE, GLOUCESTERSHIRE

There has been a castle at Sudeley, close to Winchcombe, since the eleventh century. It was rebuilt in the mid-fifteenth century by the Lancastrian, Ralph Boteler. King Edward IV, a Yorkist, forced Boteler to sell the castle to him and it remained in royal hands until 1547, when it was given to Sir Thomas Seymour, brother to Queen Jane Seymour, the third wife of Henry VIII. After Henry's death in 1547, his sixth and last wife Catherine Parr married Sir Thomas, bringing her court to Sudeley Castle. She died in childbirth a year later and is buried in the castle chapel of St Mary's. During the Civil War the castle changed hands many times before the Royalists were eventually defeated by the Parliamentarians. The Elizabethan banqueting hall was reduced to ruins and the chapel desecrated. St Mary's was restored in 1862 by Sir Gilbert Scott and the castle partly rebuilt.

NAUNTON,
GLOUCESTERSHIRE

The River Windrush is an attractive feature of the upland village of Naunton, or 'Niwetone' as it is called in Domesday Book. Although hidden at the backs of the houses and crossed by tiny stone footbridges, there is a footpath that leads along the river bank towards the church, passing the site of what may once have been a mill. Naunton was an important site for the quarrying of slate and supplied millions of stone tiles for the roofs of Oxford colleges. In the fields around the village numerous ancient coins and arrowheads have been found, but the most remarkable discovery was the fossilized print of a Chinese ginko tree leaf, 250 million years old. From Naunton the river meanders in lazy coils between rush banks, passing under Harford Bridge and down the wooded valley to Fosse Bridge, near Bourton-on-the-Water.

NAUNTON,
GLOUCESTERSHIRE

Naunton is a tiny village strung out along the River Windrush for nearly a mile. The church of St Andrew stands on a knoll at the western end of the village and contains a delicately carved stone pulpit, dating from the fourteenth century. Cromwell House, built in the village at the beginning of the seventeenth century, was owned by the Aylworth family, who are remembered by a small hamlet that bears their name, a mile south of Naunton. Richard Aylworth, a Parliamentarian, fought in the final battle of the first Civil War when the King's forces were defeated near Stow-on-the-Wold in 1644. To the north and south of Naunton the wolds are still sheep country.

TEMPLE GUITING WOLD, GLOUCESTERSHIRE

The building of a dry-stone wall is a craft that dates back to prehistoric times. The Stone Age people who built the ancient long barrows, found throughout the Cotswolds, were extremely skilful in the use of stone. At Belas Knap (near Winchcombe), for example, stones less than an inch thick have been fitted together so accurately that it would be difficult to insert the blade of a knife between. If stones are not laid down on a wall in the same way as they were in the quarry then, after a severe frosty winter, they will begin to flake and crumble and eventually the wall will collapse. The walls are traditionally topped by 'combers', large stones standing upright, to protect the courses below from getting too wet.

KINETON, GLOUCESTERSHIRE

Although a large number of corn mills were built in the Cotswolds immediately after the Norman Conquest, the earliest reference to a fulling mill appears in 1185, when the Knights Templar held two at Barton, near Kineton, a mile or so south of Temple Guiting. Temple Guiting takes its name from the Templars, who owned the manor there in the twelfth century, and from the Old English name for the upper Windrush, *gyte*, meaning 'gush' or 'flood'. The river flows south from Temple Guiting, through a deep wooded valley to the tiny hamlet of Kineton, where it is crossed by two fords. It passes under an ancient 'clapper' stone bridge before continuing to Barton and Guiting Power, where it curves south-eastwards to be joined by the Dikler near Bourton-on-the-Water.

CIRENCESTER, GLOUCESTERSHIRE

The Romans invaded Britain in
AD 43 and within a few years
had founded *Corinium
Dobunnorum*, beside the River
Churn, as an administrative
centre for the Dobunni tribe.
The Saxons destroyed the town
in the sixth century, changing its
name back to *Coryn Ceastre*, or
Cirencester. The Normans built
a great abbey here, which was
demolished at the Dissolution.
In medieval times the town
became a major centre for wool,
and it has a magnificent 'wool'
church, which stands beside the
market square. The parish
church of St John the Baptist is
one of the largest in England,
indeed larger than many British
cathedrals. The tower was built
in the fifteenth century. It rises
to 162 feet and was originally
intended to carry a spire. The
unique three-storey south porch
was the administrative centre of
the medieval abbey and later
served as the Town Hall.

CIRENCESTER, GLOUCESTERSHIRE

Radiating from the Market
Place, with its Victorian Corn
Hall, is a network of small
streets that still preserve many
of the buildings of the ancient
town. Thomas Street contains
the fifteenth-century Weavers'
Hall Almshouses. Coxwell
Street has an unspoilt row of
wool-merchants' houses and
weavers' cottages. There is a
Norman Gatehouse in Grove
Lane and in nearby Spitalgate
are the remains of the Hospital
and the Chantry of St John the
Evangelist, founded in the
twelfth century. Dollar Street,
or 'Dole Hall Street', was where
the wealthy abbots distributed
money and gifts to the poor.
Silver Street, Castle Street,
Blackjack Street, Park Street and
Cecily Hill, all have buildings of
interest. From the top of the
church tower the view to the
west reveals Cirencester Park.
The park belongs to Lord
Bathurst whose eighteenth-
century mansion, is hidden from
the town by one of the highest
yew hedges in the world.

COTSWOLD FARM PARK,
GLOUCESTERSHIRE

Cotswold Sheep, known as
'Cotswold Lions', are a large
and ancient breed of sheep,
particularly noted for their long
wool, which brought great
wealth to the region in the
Middle Ages. Introduced by the
Romans, they thrived on the
rich herbage of the limestone
wolds and their numbers
increased to thousands. William
Camden wrote at the end of the
sixteenth century: 'Upon these
hills are fed large flocks of sheep
with whitish wool, having long
necks and square bodies.'
Cotswold sheep are large-
boned, heavy-fleeced animals
with wide heads that should,
traditionally, have forelocks left
unsheared. Today they are
extremely rare due to the
increased use of synthetic fabrics
and the demand for a small joint
with a minimum of fat.

BIRDLIP HILL,
GLOUCESTERSHIRE

The Roman Ermin Way ran in a
north-westerly direction from
Silchester to Cirencester and
across the Cotswolds to Birdlip
Hill, where it zig-zagged in a
sharp descent down the Edge
into the vale to Gloucester. Prior
to 1675 the hill had been called
'Brydelepe', or Bride-leap. To
the north of the hill, in an Iron
Age burial mound at Barrow
Wake, was discovered the
superbly worked bronze Birdlip
Mirror, now preserved in
Gloucester Museum. At
Cooper's Hill, to the west, on
Spring Bank Holiday Monday
there is held an annual
cheese-rolling competition,
where contestants chase cheeses
down the slope and are allowed
to keep any that they catch.

COTSWOLD FARM PARK, GLOUCESTERSHIRE

Oxen are castrated male cattle of any breed and were used for heavy work on the light hill soils of the Cotswolds. They worked in teams to plough or pull carts and, until the beginning of the twentieth century, they were the main source of power in agriculture. The Longhorn is now a rare breed of cattle. They are direct descendants of the wild cattle that were domesticated by prehistoric man. They were extremely popular until about 1800 when they were superceded by the Shorthorn. The Cotswold Farm Park, at Bemborough Farm, is the centre of the Rare Breeds Survival Trust, where many endangered species of domesticated animals are bred and preserved. It was established in 1970, European Conservation Year.

TADDINGTON WOLD, GLOUCESTERSHIRE

The valley of the Windrush begins at Oat Hill, 921 feet above sea level, and etches its way south through the high windswept wolds towards Cutsdean. The river itself bubbles out of the hillside at Field Barn, Taddington, which in a dry summer is little more than a patch of damp ground. Within a few miles of its source the Windrush is joined by several springs and quickly becomes a stream. It is the largest of the Cotswold rivers, yet from Taddington to the Thames it covers only thirty miles. For most of its journey it travels through unspoilt countryside with dense woods and open meadows separating the villages and towns. The headwaters of the Windrush rise in the least populated area of wold country with isolated farmsteads and very few villages. This was the original 'Cotswolds', until the term grew to embrace a very much larger area.

THE SHIPTONS, GLOUCESTERSHIRE

A small headwater of the Coln rises on the wild, uninhabited wolds near Hampen to wind its way down a steep and twisting valley, passing Shipton, Shipton Oliffe and Shipton Solers. Shipton, meaning 'sheep farmstead', suggests that sheep rearing went on here long before the Norman Conquest. According to Domesday Book Shipton was divided into two manors, Oliffe and Solers, each with its own church. In 1776 they were united as one parish, but still retain their former identities. The tiny stream that flows through each of the villages, tumbling over watersplashes and little falls on its way to the Coln, is crossed by footbridges and a ford. In places the banks have dry-stone walls and, in summer, the water sparkles with the reflected brilliance of mimulus.

CHEDWORTH ROMAN VILLA, GLOUCESTERSHIRE

In 1864 a gamekeeper, digging a lost ferret out of a rabbit warren, unearthed fragments of mosaic. Excavations at the site revealed the well-preserved remains of a Romano-British villa, one of the finest in Britain. It was built in the first century AD and was occupied for nearly 400 years. The villa was situated in a sheltered position at the head of a beautiful wooded coomb, overlooking the Coln valley. Lord Eldon, who owned the property and financed the excavation of the site in 1864–6, built the mock Tudor house and museum, which contains a fascinating collection of household objects. There are several mosaics, made from local materials, and one, depicting the four seasons, is extremely well preserved. Chedworth villa is close to two ancient roads: the prehistoric White Way and the Fosse Way, both meeting in the south at Cirencester. It belongs to the National Trust.

HAZLETON WOLD,
GLOUCESTERSHIRE

The characteristics of the high wolds are subtle, not dramatic. The limestone has been weathered to a smooth surface, with gentle undulations that are open to the sky. It is a landscape that changes constantly, dependant on sun, wind and cloud to create an infinite variety of textures, patterns, colours and moods. The light soil is poor, yet it manages to support grass, crops, flowers and trees. In the area around Turkdean the pasture has been turned into arable land, where fields of wheat, barley and oats are grown. The scarcity of water on the high wolds led to tightly packed, stone-built villages, usually grouped around the manor or church. Notgrove, Hazleton and Turkdean are good examples.

WISTLEY HILL,
GLOUCESTERSHIRE

In recent years new crops have had a colourful and dramatic effect on the landscape of the wolds. Fields of yellow oilseed rape, grown to provide oil for the food industry, are now widespread. While sunflowers, planted for oil and animal feed, are becoming established. This field of sunflowers is near a busy crossroads, where the River Churn rises in a small dell known as Seven Springs. There is a rival claim that Seven Springs is in fact the source of the River Thames. This claim was discussed in the House of Commons in 1937, when the Minister of Agriculture, W. S. Morrison, member for Cirencester and Tewkesbury, concluded: 'that the River Thames rises in my constituency and not that of my Honourable Friend.' However, a plaque at Seven Springs bears the Latin inscription: *HIC TUUS O TAMESINE PATER SEPTEMGEMINUS*, or 'Here, O Father Thames, thy sevenfold spring'.

BURFORD AND THE EASTERN WOLDS

Five Cotswold rivers – the Evenlode, Windrush, Leach, Coln and Churn – rise on the high wolds to flow south to join the Thames. Three – the Frome, Little Avon and Bristol Avon – flow west to join the Severn. There are many minor tributaries feeding these rivers and, in the north, a few rivers flow into the Warwickshire Avon and the Stour.

Apart from the Frome, running through the 'Golden Valley' to Stroud, the main rivers have escaped industrialization, remaining clear, sparkling and secretive for much of their journeys. The Windrush is the longest of the truly Cotswold rivers. Yet it covers only thirty miles from its source, near Cutsdean, to the Thames.

The Evenlode is the most easterly of the rivers, rising near Moreton-in-Marsh to meander down a broad and wooded valley between Stow-on-the-Wold and Chipping Norton. It passes the remnants of the once great Forest of Wychwood before entering the Thames near Oxford.

In the Eastern Wolds both the Coln and the Leach lend their names to a string of delightful villages that lie along their course: Coln St Dennis, Coln Rogers, Coln St Aldwyns, Eastleach Martin, Eastleach Turville and the market town of Northleach, with its magnificent 'wool' church.

Seven Springs, high on the western Edge, gives birth to the Churn, which winds down a densely wooded valley past Colesbourne, Chedworth Roman Villa, North Cerney and Bagendon (the capital of the British Dobunni tribe) to Cirencester. Although it becomes part of the Thames near Cricklade, there are some who claim that its source is really that of the Thames. It was debated in the House of Commons and, although the source at Seven Springs is further from the mouth of the Thames than its official source at Thames Head, near Cirencester, the claim was dismissed.

It is to the Eastern Wolds that all these central rivers turn.

FAIRFORD,
GLOUCESTERSHIRE

There has been a corn mill on the Coln at Fairford since the Norman Conquest, perhaps earlier. By the end of the thirteenth century it was fulling cloth for the wool merchants of the town. The deep-gabled millhouse that stands on the edge of the town today was built in the seventeenth century and has now been converted into holiday homes for tourists.

FILKINS,
OXFORDSHIRE

A few miles due east of Eastleach Martin is Filkins, just over the border in Oxfordshire. The main Burford to Swindon road once passed right through the village. But now, thanks to a bypass, walking along its tranquil streets is like stepping into the past. For here, on the eastern edge of the wolds, many of the age-old Cotswold crafts have been revived. At the end of the village in an eighteenth-century stone barn the looms are working again. Here the Cotswold Woollen Weavers card, spin and weave the wool using traditional methods and machinery. There is also a museum. But the most outstanding feature of this unique village is the stone. Every cottage, from floor to roof, is built of the local stone and, unusually, so are the garden walls. Looking more like gravestones than fences, these thin slabs, or 'planks', of stone were fastened with iron ties made by the local blacksmith.

BIBURY,
GLOUCESTERSHIRE

'The most beautiful village in England', was how William Morris described Bibury, situated below the tree-lined slopes of the Coln valley. Here the river flows fast and wide, running alongside the main street. On the other side of the river is Rack Isle, a watermeadow (now a wildfowl sanctuary) where wool was once hung on racks to dry after it had been washed in Arlington Row. This famous row of stone cottages dates from the early seventeenth century. They were the homes of weavers who supplied cloth to the fulling mill, a few hundred yards downstream, with its massive stone buttresses. Arlington Row and Rack Isle are owned by the National Trust.

BURFORD,
OXFORDSHIRE

From the Barringtons the Windrush flows eastwards, through willow-hung watermeadows and under a triple-arched, low stone bridge, towards Burford Church with its graceful steeple. The church of St John the Baptist is situated in the oldest part of the town, where a small settlement grew up about a ford at which a number of ancient ways crossed – most importantly the direct route that led from Stow-on-the-Wold to the upper reaches of the Thames. There are some magnificent stone monuments in the churchyard. Near the church door there is a group of curious barrel-vaulted tombs, known as 'bale-tombs' because of their resemblance to bales of wool tied round with cords. It is said that when the people of Burford lost their right to hunt deer in the nearby Forest of Wychwood, the poachers hid their unlawfully gained venison inside the tombs.

BURFORD,
OXFORDSHIRE

Popularly referred to as 'The Gateway to the Cotswolds', Burford's wide, steep, main street leads northwards down through the town to the River Windrush, where the buildings abruptly stop. Here the road narrows, crosses an old stone bridge and climbs up Westhall Hill on to the wolds. In the Middle Ages Burford was a major wool town, but, unlike Cirencester, Fairford, North-leach or Minchinhampton, it has no central market square. Trading was carried on in the wide street, and the twin-gabled 'Tolsey' (or Market Hall), used for collecting tolls, still survives, although it is now a museum. Burford has a variety of stone and half-timbered buildings, dating from the thirteenth century, which make attractive use of the local natural resources: timber (from the once extensive Forest of Wychwood) and stone. Burford stone was also taken by river to Oxford and London for buildings such as Blenheim Palace and St Paul's Cathedral.

FAIRFORD,
GLOUCESTERSHIRE

The 'wool' church of St Mary dominates this ancient market town, situated at a river-crossing on the edge of the Cotswolds, almost in the Thames valley. The church was built around the beginning of the sixteenth century by John Tame, a wealthy wool and cloth merchant, who – in twenty-eight unique stained-glass windows – tried to portray, for the mainly illiterate congregation, a pictorial summary of the Christian faith. These fabulous windows, known as 'the poor man's bible', retain their original stained and painted glass and are said to rank among the finest in England. For more than 400 years they have survived war and religious strife, being removed on a number of occasions, notably during the Civil War and World War II. Even without the windows, however, the church is worthy of attention: built in Perpendicular style, beautifully proportioned, it is adorned with a wealth of medieval carving.

WINDRUSH,
GLOUCESTERSHIRE

The Windrush is the largest of the Cotswold rivers. By contrast, the village that bears its name is tiny. It clings to a steep slope above the valley to the south-west of Barrington Park, at the point where the river changes its direction from south to east. The houses and cottages are built of local stone, mined out of the hillside below. The village is situated round a triangular green, shaded by lime trees, with the church of St Peter commanding the highest ground. Its impressive south doorway is Norman and features a double row of fantastic, beak-headed demons with strange staring eyes – warning the worshipper that he who hesitates in crossing the portal is lost. The church and the village are monuments to the skill of the local stonemasons: from the magnificent bale-tombs to the superbly carved windows and doorways of the houses and cottages.

EASTLEACH MARTIN, GLOUCESTERSHIRE

The Leach flows south-east from Northleach, past the village of Eastington, from where it winds through parkland, meadows and woods, passes under what was once the great Roman Akeman Street, and enters Eastleach Martin and Eastleach Turville. The villages, situated on opposite banks of the river, are connected by an old stone 'clapper' footbridge, known as Keble's Bridge. It was thought to have been built by John Keble, writer of religious verse, who must have crossed the river many times when he was rector of both parish churches here in 1815. Hidden behind the trees is the tiny church of St Michael and St Martin, and facing it across the wide sparkling water is St Andrew's. It is on this beautiful stretch of the River Leach that the rare dipper can be found: a bird that has the curious ability to walk underwater along the beds of fast-flowing streams in search of food.

NORTHLEACH, GLOUCESTERSHIRE

Like Stow-on-the-Wold, Northleach is not only situated just off the Fosse Way but was also a great market town: famous throughout Europe for its wool. Its fifteenth-century church of St Peter and St Paul was built by the wealthy merchants, in Perpendicular style, and embellished with beautifully carved stonework. It contains many fine memorial brasses, depicting the church's benefactors together with the sheep and woolsacks that made them so rich. The battlemented tower, 100 feet high, overlooks the market square and dominates the surrounding countryside. In the seventeenth century the wool trade declined when the spinners and weavers left to work in the mechanized Stroud valley, whose rivers had more power than the weak-flowing Leach to drive the mill-wheels.

LITTLE BARRINGTON, GLOUCESTERSHIRE

Little Barrington was the home of the Strong family, whose fame as master masons and suppliers of limestone for some of the finest houses in the Cotswolds was enhanced by the rebuilding of London after the Great Fire of 1666. It was Thomas Strong who, under the direction of Christopher Wren, laid the foundation stone of St Paul's Cathedral. The stone for the village of Little Barrington came out of a large depression nearby where a small stream wells up. It is now a wild, though attractive, grass- and reed-covered hollow. Cottages form a large oval around the rim, broken only by the road running through. The stone from the quarries was shipped in flat-bottomed barges down the Windrush. On the north side of the village are the remains of an old sloping weir where the water level could be raised to enable the laden barges to avoid the mill-race below.

LITTLE FARINGDON, OXFORDSHIRE

'When does the may-fly come, the gorgeous succulent may-fly, that we all love so well in the quiet valleys where the trout streams wend their silent ways?' asked J. Arthur Gibbs. The year the photograph was taken, they came on a still, warm, sunny afternoon in the first week of June. No longer glass-smooth, the waters of the Leach boiled with fish. The air was alive with glistening, flying insects: the males of which were consumed by a frantic urge to mate before they died. The instant their delicate wings touched the water, invisible mouths rose silently from beneath the reeds to snap them up, exploding on the surface in a turmoil of excitement. The old stone mill (the last before Lechlade, where the Leach joins the Thames) is now a house, overlooking the well-stocked ponds of a trout farm. Here the land is flat and, on both sides of the raised Burford to Lechlade road, the river floods to form a wide and treeless lake. The tiny hamlet of Little Faringdon is about a mile away by road, to the north-east.

STROUD AND THE GOLDEN VALLEYS

Throughout the Cotswolds many people were engaged in the small-scale production of cloth: from the cottage weavers with their hand looms to the landowners with their fulling mills, the earliest recorded mill being the one at Barton, near Temple Guiting, owned by the Knights Templar in the twelfth century. But, by the end of the sixteenth century, the major centre for the cloth industry was in the Stroud valleys, whence vast quantities of cloth were exported to Europe.

The reason for this development was two-fold: the area was rich in fuller's earth, used in the clothmaking process, and there were abundant supplies of pure, soft, fast-flowing water for washing and dyeing the cloth and for powering the mills.

Five valleys converge on Stroud: Painswick, Slad, Chalford, Toadsmoor and Nailworth. All have fast-flowing streams and all were actively involved in clothmaking, creating so much wealth for the clothiers that they came to be known as the 'Golden Valleys'. The largest is the Chalford valley, where the River Frome runs down the bottom of a deep narrow gorge from Sapperton to Stroud. In this valley alone there were over thirty mills stretching down to the Vale of Berkeley and the Severn. The mills were sited beside the stream with the weavers' cottages clinging to the terraced slopes above, and narrow, winding lanes allowing only enough room for the to-ing and fro-ing of pack-animals.

A few miles to the south, Dursley, tucked in under the dark slopes of Stinchcombe Hill and at the mouth of the Uley valley, also prospered from the cloth industry.

The process of turning the fleece into cloth involved many stages. The raw wool was initially sorted, in terms of quality and length, and washed. At this stage it may well have been dyed or bleached, or this may have been left until later. After dying, the wool was thoroughly oiled before it was carded or combed to loosen the fibres for spinning. Until machinery for spinning had been installed in the mills, the wool was generally spun in the cottages. The yarn, which varied in thickness according to the product, was reeled into skeins in readiness for weaving. The type of loom used depended on the sort of cloth that was to be produced and many weavers' houses and cottages were built with a room or

OWLPEN, GLOUCESTERSHIRE

Owlpen is a unique and secret place, hidden in a wooded coomb, less than a mile east of Uley. There has been a settlement here from Saxon times at least, probably because of the clear springs that flow into the Ewelme stream. The village, built entirely of Cotswold stone, is grouped around the three-gabled Tudor manor house and includes a Court House, a massive barn, a mill and a church.

attic wide enough to accommodate the loom frame. After the wool had been woven into an open mesh it was taken to the mill where it was scoured to remove the oil and thoroughly examined for flaws before being 'fulled'. Prior to the development of the fulling mill, the method used to shrink and thicken the cloth was long and laborious: a process that involved 'walkers' or 'tuckers' treading the cloth underfoot in an alkaline solution for hours. In the mills, however, heavy wooden mallets, powered by a water-wheel, slowly pounded the fabric in water and the yellow clay known as fuller's earth. The thick shrunken cloth was then roughened with teasel heads, set in a metal frame. The raised surface of the cloth was sheared smooth and the material was ready for dying and finishing.

During the sixteenth century most of the cloth was exported immediately after it had been fulled; undyed and unfinished. But, with the expansion of world markets, particular areas became famous for certain colours: for example, Uley blues and blacks; Stroud reds and scarlets.

As the wool trade declined the cloth trade prospered, producing large fortunes for the clothiers, some of whom used their wealth to marry into the aristocracy, purchasing manors and houses from the ancient landowners. The lesser clothiers, with all their money tied up in their businesses, lived precariously: rich one day, poor the next. While the weavers, spinners, tuckers and others, worked long hours in unhealthy conditions for next to nothing.

By the beginning of the nineteenth century, steam power had replaced water power and, unable or unwilling to adapt, the Cotswold cloth industry came to an end.

BALL'S GREEN, GLOUCESTERSHIRE

The wolds, to the south of Minchinhampton, are densely wooded with narrow lanes that zig-zag their way up and down the landscape. Ball's Green is famous for its high-quality stone, which was used in the Houses of Parliament and Gloucester Cathedral. The farmhouse here stands on the edge of Gatcombe Wood. Nearby Gatcombe Park was built in the eighteenth century for Edward Sheppard, a rich cloth merchant; it is now the home of Princess Anne.

PAINSWICK,
GLOUCESTERSHIRE

Painswick is an old market town of silver-grey stone buildings that date back to the fourteenth century. It was a major centre of the cloth industry for almost 300 years, until production declined in the nineteenth century. The former prosperity of the town is reflected in many fine houses and mansions, including eighteenth-century Painswick House, the gabled Court House and seventeenth-century Castle Hale. Earlier buildings worthy of note are the ancient half-timbered Post Office and the Little Fleece, owned by the National Trust. The churchyard of St Mary's is famous for its ninety-nine ancient yews that are said to be uncountable. In 1883 a bolt of lightning struck the church spire, bringing a huge section of it crashing down on the nave roof and damaging many of the magnificent table tombs.

PAINSWICK,
GLOUCESTERSHIRE

Just as surely as if it were gold, the water that tumbles down the steep slopes around Painswick brought great wealth and prosperity to the town. It was the clear, fast-flowing streams – ideal for powering the fulling mills – that attracted the cloth industry, beginning with the arrival, in the sixteenth century, of a colony of Flemish weavers who settled in the town. There was also stone in the surrounding hills, in abundance, and with it the weavers built mills (as many as thirty by 1820), a magnificent hill town, and a silver-grey church with a soaring steeple. Even though the mills have long ceased production, Painswick stands proudly on the hillside with all the dignity expected from the, once great, 'Queen of the Cotswolds'.

SAPPERTON,
GLOUCESTERSHIRE

After the Industrial Revolution the depopulated (and then remote) villages in the Cotswolds attracted a number of craftsmen and artists. Sapperton attracted a group who, inspired by the hopes and ideals of William Morris, dedicated themselves 'to purity of design and first-class workmanship'. When Ernest Gimson and the Barnsley brothers came to the village towards the end of the nineteenth century, they established a workshop and showroom in the fourteenth-century manor, Daneway House. Within a few short years they had created a thriving community of fine craftsmen, which included blacksmiths, wheelwrights and furniture-makers.
Unfortunately, on Gimson's death in 1919 the workshop had to close and the group dispersed. Gimson is buried, along with the Barnsley brothers, high on the hillside, in the cemetery of the little gabled church of St Kenelm.

MINCHINHAMPTON,
GLOUCESTERSHIRE

On a tongue of high land, between the 'Golden Valley' and the Nailsworth valley, is the small hilltop town of Minchinhampton. After the Norman Conquest, the town was given to a convent at Caen in Normandy. The convent owned large flocks of sheep that grazed on the high and lush pasture and, by the thirteenth century, Minchinhampton was an important market town. The market square, to which the narrow streets lead, has a Market House, supported on stone pillars, which was erected in 1698. By the beginning of the eighteenth century it was not only a major centre for wool and cloth but also for fine-quality stone, which was quarried nearby. The town itself is built of grey stone. Attempting to soar above the houses, but unable to do so because of its curious truncated spire, is the church of Holy Trinity. Dame Alys Hampton gave the townsfolk Minchin-hampton Common, 'to belong to them for ever'. It is now owned by the National Trust.

SLAD VALLEY, GLOUCESTERSHIRE

In 1959 Laurie Lee immortalized the village of Slad in *Cider with Rosie*. The memories he so vividly recalled of his childhood days magically linger on: in his handsome house, a seventeenth-century stone cottage standing on a steep bank above the lake; in the grey-stone village, scattered along the south-east slope of the narrow valley, with its church, schoolhouse, mill and pub; in the squire's house, called Steanbridge, built in Elizabethan times with eighteenth-century additions. It was one of a number of cloth mills driven by the stream that winds and twists down the valley towards Stroud. Within the parish of Painswick, the Slad valley was a centre of clothmaking until the nineteenth century, when the mills ceased production: Steanbridge in 1825, Hazel Mill in 1870 and New Mills in 1897. The inn, The Woolpack, situated in the centre of the village, stands as a reminder of its history.

CHALFORD, GLOUCESTERSHIRE

Chalford, perched on the precipitous slopes of the 'Golden Valley', has been described as 'a truly Alpine village'. It was an industrial centre, its water-powered mills grinding corn and fulling cloth long before the Industrial Revolution brought even greater prosperity to the region. It was through this busy valley that the cloth was transported from Stroud to London for export overseas. At the end of the eighteenth century a canal, running beside the River Frome and through a two-mile tunnel at Sapperton further up the valley, linked the Severn to the Thames. It was superseded by the railways and, in a state of disrepair, was finally closed in 1933. Fortunately, the demise of the water-powered cloth industry in the Cotswolds left this valley not as a scarred wasteland, but with many small and attractive buildings that have now become the homes and workshops of local craftsmen.

CAM VALLEY,
GLOUCESTERSHIRE

Uleybury Hillfort commands an impressive strategic position on a high ridge that overlooks, to the east and south, the Cam valley and, to the west, a view that extends across the Severn plain to the Black Mountains of Wales. The small hillock is Cam Long Down and, in the distance, the dark curve of the Edge reaches its most westerly point at Stinchcombe Hill, above Dursley. Enclosing thirty-two acres of hill-top, Uleybury is one of the largest Iron Age forts in the Cotswolds and there is evidence that the Romans made use of it. Less than a mile north of the fort is Hetty Pegler's Tump, an ancient long barrow – 120 feet by 22 feet – with five burial chambers (two have been sealed off) constructed of large stone slabs with dry-stone walling. Excavations in 1854 unearthed fifteen skeletons.

BISLEY,
GLOUCESTERSHIRE

The Frome rises high on the western escarpment, near Birdlip, and sweeps in a semicircle around an isolated plateau to Stroud. In the centre of this plateau is Bisley, nearly 800 feet above sea level. Seven springs gush from the hillside into a lane by the churchyard. Known as Bisley Wells, they were restored in 1863 by Thomas Keble, vicar of All Saints Church and brother of John, famous for his book of sacred verse, *The Christian Year*. The springs, believed to have special healing properties, have been sacred for thousands of years. There is evidence that the Romans worshipped at altars here and a statue of Mars was discovered nearby. Even now, on Ascension Day, children dress the well-heads with flowers after a service in the church. Wesley House – connected with John Wesley, co-founder of the Methodist movement – dates from the sixteenth century.

DURSLEY,
GLOUCESTERSHIRE

Nestling under the dark, northern slopes of Stinchcombe Hill, Dursley was an important market town and clothmaking centre in the eighteenth century. The elegant, two-storeyed Market Hall, supported on stone pillars and arches with a recessed statue of Queen Anne, was built in 1738. The statue commemorates the Queen's financial donation towards the repair of the church spire, which collapsed in 1698 while the bells were being rung, killing several ringers. The Church of St James dates from the fifteenth century and contains a fourteenth-century stone font. With the decline of the Cotswold woollen industry many of the mills were converted into light-engineering factories. Listers of Dursley, established in the 1860s, prospered and survives, making engines and agricultural machinery.

CAM LONG DOWN,
GLOUCESTERSHIRE

Cam Long Down is an island hill situated in the centre of the semicircular sweep of escarpment (broken only by the Cam valley) that begins at Frocester Hill, in the north-east, and ends at Stinchcombe Hill, in the south-west. Although the Edge here is thick with beech woods – where foxes and badgers thrive and the wood warbler sings its shivering song in spring – Cam Long Down is almost treeless. The slopes of the conical-shaped Cam Peak are clothed in waist-high bracken, while on the summit is close-cropped turf. The peak was created, according to legend, by the devil who, intending to dam the Severn with a gigantic wheelbarrowful of Cotswold stone, was tricked by a cobbler into dumping his load here. Cam lies at the foot of Cam Peak and its mill, still working, was the only one in the Dursley area to survive the demise of the Cotswold cloth industry.

STROUD,
GLOUCESTERSHIRE

It was Stroud's position at the convergence of five valleys that made it the industrial centre of the Cotswolds in the seventeenth century. By the early nineteenth century there were 150 fulling mills in the main valley, which became known as the Golden Valley because of the wealth it generated for the cloth merchants. The town's prosperity declined with the competition from the improved efficiency of steam power and, although a few mills adapted and survived, the rest fell silent – until new industries were established in place of the old. Six hundred feet above and to the south of the town is Rodborough Common, 242 acres of bleak, uncultivated pasture, pockmarked with the remains of Stone Age long barrows and Iron Age earthworks. Rodborough and nearby Minchinhampton Common are both owned by the National Trust.

NAILSWORTH,
GLOUCESTERSHIRE

The Nailsworth Avon rises near Cherington, passing through Avening, Gatcombe Wood and Longford's Mill, before it is joined by a small stream at Nailsworth: a clothmaking town, situated at the foot of a deep wooded valley with houses spilling down the hillsides. In its heyday Nailsworth was a prosperous town with many mills. Egypt Mill and Day's Mill each had two water-wheels, operated by ponds placed side by side. Dunkirk Mill had as many as five water-wheels, driven by a powerful leat, fifteen feet wide. It was this mill that is thought to be described by Mrs Dinah Maria Craik in her novel *John Halifax, Gentleman*, which she wrote at Amberley, nearby. The roads around Nailsworth are steep and one, which consists of a series of particularly treacherous bends, is popularly known as the Nailsworth Ladder.

BATH AND THE SOUTHWOLDS

Over 7,000 years ago the Cotswolds were covered with a dense forest that stretched from the east to the western escarpment, spilling down the slopes to continue across the Severn valley to the Black Mountains of Wales and beyond. The earliest people to inhabit these forested wolds were nomadic hunters, travelling by way of the less-wooded hilltops and ridges.

Between 5,000 and 6,000 BC the first settlers arrived and began to exploit the natural resources of the forest. These Mesolithic groups of hunters and food-gatherers built camps and established their territorial hunting grounds throughout the length and breadth of the wolds, as the discovery of numerous flint implements has proved.

They were followed, in about 3,000 BC, by the Neolithic people, who cleared the hilltops of trees to build barrows, or burial mounds, like Belas Knap, near Winchcombe, and Hetty Pegler's Tump, near Uley. They were the first farmers, cultivating the soil to grow crops to feed themselves and their livestock. It was a development that not only changed the face of the landscape, but revolutionized the way of life of early man. Farming enabled meat and grain to be stored, providing greater security of food supplies. The existence of a surplus meant that there was more leisure time for other activities. Cultural and technological advances followed, leading to larger settlements, more permanent buildings and the invention of pottery and metallurgy.

Working with metal is one of the oldest of Cotswold crafts. From the excavations of burial mounds there is evidence that the Iron Age metal-workers had a sophisticated knowledge of the technical processes involved in extracting one metal from another. At Barrow Wake, near Birdlip, a superbly worked bronze mirror, decorated with coloured enamels, a silver-gilt brooch and a bronze animal-headed dagger were discovered.

The Iron Age people took advantage of the many promontories to build defensive hill-forts, the greatest number being sited along the Edge. When the Romans invaded Britain in the first century AD, they quickly established a frontier along the line of these hill-forts, linking them with major military roads like the Fosse Way, Ermin Way and Akeman Street. Situated at their intersection, *Corinium Dobunnorum* (Cirencester)

TOR HILL,
GLOUCESTERSHIRE

The hilltops above Wotton-under-Edge have been farmed for centuries. Although today the fields are ploughed by tractors, it was not so long ago that a standard team of eight oxen was used. The furrows were long, due to the difficulty of turning the animals at the furrow's end.

became the capital of the region, with *Aquae Sulis* (Bath) guarding the southernmost tip of the limestone hills. Romano-British settlements sprung up all over the wolds with luxurious villas, like Chedworth and Woodchester, nestling on the slopes of secluded wooded valleys, close to water for drinking and bathing. Much of the land was used for grazing: the low-lying areas for cattle and the hillsides for sheep. In addition to the usual cereal and root crops, vineyards were planted on sheltered south-facing slopes.

In the seventh century, after the Roman legions had withdrawn, the Saxons took over existing settlements or established new ones of their own. They introduced heavy iron tools for felling woodland and iron ploughshares. On Wotton Hill, now owned by the National Trust, there are the remains of Anglo-Saxon 'strip lynchets', or ploughed terraces.

Gradually, over the centuries the higher and gentler wolds yielded to the plough, where teams of oxen were preferred to horses because they were cheaper to feed. They continued to be used until the 1920s, when mechanization took over.

The Industrial Revolution had little effect on the appearance of the Cotswold landscape. It was the move towards more effective farming, leading to the Enclosure Acts of the eighteenth and nineteenth centuries, that brought about the major change. The land was concentrated into fewer hands and divided by dry-stone walls, stretching for mile after mile across the wolds.

The landscape was further affected by the squires who, in the interests of fox-hunting and shooting, planted coverts. In the Southwolds a notable example is Beaufort Hunt country, between Wotton-under-Edge and Bath.

WOTTON-UNDER-EDGE, GLOUCESTERSHIRE

The soil on the hilltops above Wotton-under-Edge is well-drained, but poor and extremely shallow. With modern farming methods, however, and improved strains of corn the yield is high and, in late summer, when the fields of wheat, oats and barley are ready for harvesting the hilltops are crowned with gold.

DYRHAM PARK,
AVON

In AD 577 Dyrham was the site of a major battle, during which the Anglo-Saxons killed three British kings, resulting in the capture of Bath, Cirencester and Gloucester and, consequently, the Cotswolds. The name Dyrham is derived from the Anglo-Saxon *Deor-hamm*, meaning 'deer enclosure'. It is recorded in the *Anglo-Saxon Chronicle*. The great manor house lies on the grassy slopes of a sheltered coomb, high on the steep escarpment, with extensive views over Bristol and the Severn plain. It was built between 1692 and 1702 by William Blathwayt, Secretary of State to William III, on the site of an earlier house belonging to his wife's family, the Wynters. The grounds were once landscaped and contained one of the most ambitious terraced water gardens in England, with statues, fountains, ornamental pools and waterfalls. The manor house and 263 acres of parkland now belong to the National Trust.

BADMINTON HOUSE,
AVON

Badminton House has been the seat of the Dukes of Beaufort for over 300 years. The house stands in 15,000 acres of wooded parkland, with herds of fallow and red deer, sheep, a lake and a Great Avenue that is several miles long. The oldest part of the house was built by Henry Somerset, Marquis of Worcester, who was made the first Duke of Beaufort in 1682. The dimensions of the hall determined the size of the badminton court, for it was here that the shuttlecock game was first played. The third Duke commissioned William Kent to enlarge and embellish the mansion and to build in the park the monumental gateway, Worcester Lodge. Badminton is world-famous for its International Horse Trials held in the park each spring, the popularity of which is enhanced by royal participation and attendance. It is also the headquarters of the Beaufort Hunt.

HORTON COURT,
AVON

Horton Court is the oldest inhabited house in the Cotswolds, with an unfortified Norman hall (built *circa* 1140) forming the north wing of the house – a rarity in a domestic building. The manor house was built in 1521 for William Knight, later Bishop of Bath and Wells. In 1527 he was sent by Henry VIII to Rome to attempt to speed up the annulment of his marriage to Catherine of Aragon. Although his mission proved to be futile, he brought back with him the idea for an Italian-style ambulatory, or loggia, to be adorned with the heads of four Roman emperors. The covered arcade was built in the garden of Horton, away from the house, with flat Gothic arches. The manor house and its church is set in a secluded hollow below an Iron Age hill-fort. It is owned by the National Trust, but only the hall and ambulatory are open to the public.

MALMESBURY,
WILTSHIRE

Malmesbury is an ancient market town, dating from the fifth century, and a place of pilgrimage since the earliest beginnings of Christianity in Britain. The town lays claim to being the oldest borough in England, having been granted its charter by King Edward, son of Alfred the Great, in 924. It is perched on a hill above the Bristol Avon. The magnificent Benedictine abbey was built by the Normans on the site of an earlier monastic building, founded in the sixth century. It survived being completely demolished at the Dissolution by William Stumpe, a rich clothier, who bought the abbey and allowed the nave to be used for divine worship. It became the parish church in 1541, but the rest of the abbey fell into decay. The south porch survived and its richly carved archway is considered to be the finest example of Norman decorative stonework in the country.

WOTTON-UNDER-EDGE,
GLOUCESTERSHIRE

The steep, wooded escarpment encircles Wotton-under-Edge like a defensive wall, with the town set on a ridge of high ground above the Severn valley. Its name is derived from the Saxon *Wudetun*, the 'farmstead in the wood'. The ancient town was destroyed by fire in the reign of King John and rebuilt to gain borough status in 1253. It was part of the vast estate of the powerful Berkeley family, who lived in Berkeley Castle a few miles to the north-west. Katherine, Lady Berkeley, founded the Wotton Grammar School in 1384, one of the earliest in the country. Thomas, the tenth Lord Berkeley (1352–1417), and his wife, Margaret, are buried in Wotton church. Inside the fourteenth-century church is an eighteenth-century organ, built by Christopher Shrider for George I and, reputedly, first played by Handel. It originally came from the church of St Martin-in-the-Fields, London.

NIBLEY KNOLL,
GLOUCESTERSHIRE

To the west of North Nibley, Berkeley Castle, in the vale of the River Severn, has been the home of the Berkeley family for centuries. Thomas, Lord Berkeley, whose tomb is in the church of St Mary the Virgin, Wotton-under-Edge, died in 1417 without leaving a male heir. Rival claims to the ownership of the Berkeley estates were disputed for years, one claimant or another seizing lands and properties in order to support their case. Eventually, in 1469, Lord Lisle challenged William, Lord Berkeley, to a dual at Nibley Green, below Nibley Knoll. Both men could each command a force of over 1,000 men and a battle ensued in which Lord Lisle was killed. It was to be the last private battle fought on English soil. The quarrel, however, continued until the seventeenth century when it was finally settled by compensation, valued at over a quarter of the Berkeley possessions.

WOTTON-UNDER-EDGE, GLOUCESTERSHIRE

Wotton-under-Edge was an ancient market town that prospered with the wool trade to become an important centre for the cloth industry. A considerable number of fulling mills were built on the springs that break out of the limestone escarpment around Wotton. Most of the streets in Wotton retain their ancient names. Market Street leads to The Chipping, originally the market place. On the corner of High Street is the Tolsey House. In Orchard Street is the house in which Isaac Pitman is said to have invented his system of shorthand in 1837. The Perry and Dawes Almshouses consist of an attractive quadrangle of seventeenth-century gabled buildings and a chapel that is entered by a small archway from Church Street. They were the gift of Hugh Perry in 1638, who was a former Sheriff of London, and extended by Thomas Dawes in the eighteenth century.

WOTTON-UNDER-EDGE, GLOUCESTERSHIRE

The fact that Wotton-under-Edge was a thriving wool-spinning and weaving town is commemorated by the sheep and teasels on the town's coat-of-arms, the carving of a woolsack over the archway of the Perry and Dawes Almshouses and by names like Shepherd's Lease, Dyer's Brook, Loom Cottage, the Shearman's Arms and the old Ram Inn. The inn is built below road level beside a small brook. It is said to have housed the masons who built the church of St Mary the Virgin in the thirteenth century. The oak-timbered, Cotswold stone building was an inn for at least 500 years, until the 1960s when it became a private house. It is reputedly haunted with at least four ghosts, including one of a priest.

TYNDALE MONUMENT,
GLOUCESTERSHIRE

Viewed from The Ridings, north-east of Wotton-under-Edge, the Tyndale Monument stands on a wooded knoll, high above the village of North Nibley. The tower, sited 650 feet above sea level and over 100 feet tall, commands a breathtaking view across the Severn plain and the Forest of Dean to the distant Black Mountains of Wales. It was erected in 1866 to the memory of William Tyndale, who first translated the Bible into English and was burnt at the stake as a heretic in 1536. Unfortunately, the William Tyndale who lived at North Nibley at the beginning of the sixteenth century may not have been the same man, whose birthplace was almost certainly somewhere 'on the borders of Wales'. The monument is reached by a steep and muddy track that ascends through beech woods, crossing a number of small hillocks, to the level turf above.

LITTLE BADMINTON,
AVON

The open countryside around Badminton is rich farmland, with dry-stone walls giving way to hedges that are entirely free of wire, for this is the territory of the Beaufort Hunt. It was the fifth Duke of Beaufort who introduced fox-hunting to the Cotswolds about 200 years ago. Today it is still popular, the Hunt meeting several times a week during the season. Beaufort country straddles the borders of Gloucestershire, Wiltshire and Avon, covering over 20,000 acres. Many of the villages and farms in the vicinity of Badminton House are part of the Beaufort estate. Little Badminton encircles the dry-stone-walled village green with stone cottages and farms, whose barns are stacked, after the harvest, with the increasingly common circular bales of hay. The stone-tiled church was once the private chapel of the early dukes of Beaufort.

TETBURY WOLD, GLOUCESTERSHIRE

It is only in the last 200 years that the wolds between Tetbury and Bath have been turned into farmland. Before the eighteenth- and nineteenth-century Enclosure Acts the landscape would have been open scrub and grassland, fit only for the grazing of sheep. Within this rough pasture, where huge flocks roamed freely, a small number of fields were cultivated on a communal basis, growing enough produce to meet local demand. The need for greater efficiency and productivity brought about the Enclosure Acts and the land was concentrated into larger farms at the expense of the smallholder. Hedgerows were grown and dry-stone walls were built and the face of the wolds changed dramatically.

OZLEWORTH BOTTOM, GLOUCESTERSHIRE

Ozleworth Bottom lies to the south-east of Wotton-under-Edge and was once a thriving valley in the seventeenth and eighteenth centuries, with fifteen fulling mills within five miles. Today its stream, which flows into the Little Avon, is tapped at its source by the Water Authority, and has been reduced to little more than a trickle. The mills have fallen into decay and everywhere is silent. The flat meadows further down the valley are ploughed or grazed by cattle and sheep, while higher up the landscape is wild. At the head of the Bottom is Ozleworth Park, laid out in the eighteenth century. Beyond the entrance gates, hidden by trees, is the little church of St Nicholas. It has a hexagonal Norman tower that is rare in the Cotswolds. Ozleworth derives its name from the Anglo-Saxon word for a blackbird and means 'blackbird frequented farm'.

OZLEWORTH BOTTOM,
GLOUCESTERSHIRE

The Cotswold escarpment around Wotton-under-Edge has been eroded by land slips and water to create a series of deep coombs that are known as the Bottoms. Tyley Bottom, Waterley Bottom and Ozleworth Bottom still retain much of their ancient woodlands, which screen many of the farms and villages from view. The area around Newark Park and Ozleworth Bottom is wild, remote and beautiful, with woods, sheltered farmland, high hedges and rough steep-sided slopes fit only for grazing. The valley is almost impenetrable, cannot be crossed and is unsuitable for vehicles, except for a single, narrow muddy lane that is dark and overhung with trees. The valley walls rise to nearly 800 feet. In places, like Hen's Cliff and Newark Park, large land slips have formed immense cliffs from which there are glorious views over the Bottoms and south-westward towards the Severn plain.

GREAT BADMINTON,
AVON

Limestone is seldom far from the surface in the Cotswolds. On the high wolds the soil is extremely shallow and after ploughing the ground is usually strewn with small broken rocks. The stone for building walls is generally quarried on site and small depressions are found near the edges of fields, where the raw material has been removed from the ground. Stone roofing slates are split from the limestone, after it has been exposed to frost, and trimmed to sizes that graduate from six inches to two feet deep. The slates are overlapped and arranged in order of size, the largest at the eaves, the smallest at the ridge. In order to support the heavy weight of the slates the roofs are steeply pitched. Because the slates are porous, the slope helps the rainwater to flow quickly away.

NEWARK PARK,
GLOUCESTERSHIRE

Newark Park stands on the edge
of a high wooded cliff
overlooking Ozleworth
Bottom. It was built by Sir
Nicholas Poyntz from the stone
of nearby Kingswood Abbey
after its demolition in the
sixteenth century. According to
tradition, all the neighbouring
churchyard and village crosses
were removed to supplement
the stone needed for this great
'new work'. It was originally an
Elizabethan hunting lodge until
1790, when it was converted
into a battlemented country
house by James Wyatt. It was
owned by the Clutterbuck
family of clothiers until 1949,
when it was given to the
National Trust along with 643
acres of woodland and farmland.
There are two other great
houses in this secluded wooded
valley: Ozleworth Park, built in
the eighteenth century, and
Boxwell Court, where Charles II
rested on his flight from the
battle of Worcester.

BEVERSTON,
GLOUCESTERSHIRE

Beverston is a village of stone
cottages and barns, a church and
the ruins of a moated castle,
which has been converted into a
private residence. The castle was
built in about 1225, on the site
of a Saxon stronghold. It was
improved a century later by
Thomas, Lord Berkeley, who,
in 1330, bought the manor of
Beverston to increase his flocks
on the Cotswolds. He added a
gatehouse and built further
accommodation in the
courtyard. During the Civil War
the castle was besieged by the
Parliamentarians. It was taken in
1644 when its Royalist
commander, Colonel
Oglethorpe, slipped out to visit
his mistress at a nearby farm and
was captured. The church of St
Mary, hidden among tall trees
beside the castle, was originally
Norman and restored in 1361.
On the south wall of the tower
is a mutilated Saxon sculpture of
the Resurrection that has also
suffered from centuries of
weathering.

TETBURY,
GLOUCESTERSHIRE

In medieval times the value of
an estate could be significantly
increased by the setting up of a
market, which, if successful,
could then be eligible for the
granting of a charter that would
allow the town where it was
held to be almost self-
governing. Tetbury laid out its
market place in the thirteenth
century and being situated at a
major crossroads – where the
Fosse Way, from Cirencester to
Bath, met the Nailsworth to
Malmesbury road – it prospered
to become an important market
town. The great wool trade of
the fifteenth and sixteenth
centuries brought further wealth
to the town and in 1655 the
Market House was built, to
which all streets lead. It stands
on twenty-one stone pillars. The
Chipping is a lesser market
square, from where the
well-worn Chipping Steps lead
down to the ancient remains of a
Cistercian priory.

HAMSWELL VALLEY,
AVON

To the north of Bath a deep
steep-sided valley cuts between
Little Solsbury Hill, the site of
an Iron Age camp, and
Lansdown Hill, where the
ancient Jurassic Way stretches to
the Humber. Tog Hill stands at
the head of the valley, with
Freezing Hill and Hanging Hill
nearby. Between them, at
Battlefields, is a massive
monument to Sir Bevil
Grenville, who was killed in the
Civil War. In 1643 he marched
with a Royalist army to attack
Bath, held by the
Parliamentarians under Sir
William Waller. Waller met
them not in the town, but on
the windswept heights of
Lansdown Hill, where a fierce
battle ensued. In his moment of
victory Grenville was wounded
and taken to Cold Ashton
Manor nearby, where he died.
The Cotswold Way from Bath
passes the battle site, drops
down into the Hamswell valley
and up to Cold Ashton, at the
beginning of its journey north to
Chipping Campden.

HILLESLEY,
AVON

Hillesley is a small village on the road from Wotton-under-Edge to Hawkesbury Upton, situated above Berkeley Hunt country in the vale and below Beaufort Hunt country on the plateau. To serve as a reminder that the village is only five miles north-west of the seat of the Beauforts at Badminton, one of the two inns, the Portcullis, bears the family crest. The two inns at nearby Hawkesbury Upton are named the Duke of Beaufort and the Fox. Above the village towers the Hawkesbury Monument, built in 1846 by Lewis Vulliamy to commemorate Lord Somerset, a member of the Beaufort family, who distinguished himself at Waterloo. It stands some 650 feet above sea level and is 120 feet tall. The villagers at Hawkesbury Upton and Hillesley built chapels for themselves. The Baptist Chapel at Hillesley was founded in 1730 and one of its earliest ministers was reputed to be a highwayman.

COLD ASHTON,
AVON

The road to the remote hill village of Cold Ashton, 650 feet above sea level, meanders up the side of the delightful St Catherine's valley. 'Cold' probably refers to its exposed position at the head of the valley where in winter the winds can be severe. In medieval times, however, the south-facing slopes supported a vineyard, where grapes were grown for wine. The gabled Cold Ashton Manor, described as one of the finest Elizabethan houses in all England, overlooks the valley and has a magnificent Renaissance gateway. The church is remarkable, not so much for its architectural merit, but for the fact that it was rebuilt in the sixteenth century at the personal expense of the Reverend Thomas Key. A small stream rises on the slopes below the village and flows down the valley to join the Bristol Avon at Bath, a few miles to the south.

CHIPPING SODBURY,
AVON

Chipping Sodbury lies at the
foot of the escarpment below
Dodington Park. As the
Chipping in its name implies, it
was an important market centre
in medieval times and stands at a
crossroads on the main route
between Bristol, Oxford and
London. Its main street, Broad
Street, is long, wide and
spacious, with the Market Cross
at one end and the church of St
John the Baptist at the other.
The stone-built town was
granted the right to hold a
market and fair in about 1227
and many of its buildings reflect
its status. There is a Tudor town
hall, a market cross, a clock
tower, together with many old
inns and fine houses. To the east
of the town, high on the
escarpment, is Old Sodbury,
with views from the churchyard
over the Severn plain towards
Bristol. Above the
fifteenth-century manor at
nearby Little Sodbury is a
massive Iron Age hill-fort.

CASTLE COMBE,
WILTSHIRE

Castle Combe nestles in a
sheltered, secluded wooded
valley to the east of the Roman
Fosse Way. In the Middle Ages
it was an important sheep and
wool centre, with a charter that
entitled the village to hold a
market and fair to which traders
were attracted from miles
around. The stone-built Market
Cross, its tiled roof supported
by pillars, is situated in the
centre of the village near the old
manor house and church. The
clothiers' houses and weavers'
cottages descend the hillside to
the By Brook, which is spanned
by a three-arched bridge. The
fast-running, trout-filled stream
flows south to join the Bristol
Avon near Bath. On the hilltop
above this lovely, unspoilt
village are prehistoric
earthworks and the remains of a
Norman castle, which gave the
village its name.

TYLEY BOTTOM,
GLOUCESTERSHIRE

Tyley Bottom's name came from the tile pits, whose remains can be found in the valley. The Saxon's called it *Tigel Leage*, or 'stone-tile quarry', and the pits may have been worked by the Romans. A tiny stream runs down the valley, which is only accessible by foot, and this is fed by many springs that issue out of the hillsides. The streams from Tyley and nearby Ozleworth Bottom were used to drive a considerable number of fulling mills that, by the eighteenth century, stretched down the valleys for miles.

LOWER KILCOTT,
AVON

The enchanting Kilcott valley runs from Barley Ridge, near Starveall, through Hennel Bottom and, at Upper Kilcott, swings north-westwards towards Hillesley, Alderley and Wotton-under-Edge. A narrow lane, which forms part of the Cotswold Way, winds leisurely down the deep valley, with a delightful stream flowing through rushes and willows alongside it. On either side the slopes are cloaked in beech woods, with fairy names like Bangel Wood, Miry Wood, Stickstey Wood and Splatt's Wood. Midger Wood is a nature reserve. There was a fulling mill in the valley at Hawkesbury in 1270, followed by many more in the next five centuries. The eighteenth-century mill at Lower Kilcott, now a private house, has much of its machinery intact. The stream flows gently into the deep millpond to rush through the narrow mill-race in a powerful current of dark and foaming water. The house is dated 1739.

BATH, AVON

Bath owes its Roman grandeur
and Georgian elegance to the hot
natural mineral springs that gush
out of the ground beside the
Bristol Avon. The Romans,
discovering the therapeutic
properties of the waters in the
first century AD, built a town,
Aquae Sulis, around the springs,
with elaborate baths and a
temple dedicated to
Sulis-Minerva: Sulis, the Celtic
goddess of the springs, and
Minerva, the Roman goddess of
healing. The town flourished for
nearly 400 years until the
Romans left Britain. The Saxon
invaders captured the town in
the sixth century. The baths,
referred to as 'the work of
giants', fell into ruin and were
soon overgrown. Although it
had long been a spa town, the
Great Bath was not uncovered
until the end of the nineteenth
century. Still partly lined with
the original Roman lead, it is fed
by springs that produce 250,000
gallons of water a day, at a
constant temperature of 49°C,
or 120°F.

BATH, AVON

Three self-made men were
responsible for Bath's
transformation into the 'golden
city': Richard 'Beau' Nash,
Ralph Allen and John Wood.
Nash came to the city in 1705
and soon became the Master of
Ceremonies, publishing and
enforcing a code of manners for
visitors. Ralph Allen became the
city's deputy postmaster in
1712, quickly rising to the
position of chief postmaster. He
made a personal fortune from
reorganizing the nation's postal
services and bought the nearby
Combe Down quarries, from
which came much of the stone
used to build Bath. John Wood
the Elder arrived in the city in
1727. He was responsible for the
design of many fine buildings,
but he died before his
masterpiece, the Circus, could
be completed. It was left to his
son, John Wood the Younger,
to carry out his father's plan.
The Royal Crescent in Victoria
Park was built by Wood the
Younger.

NORTHWICK HILL,
GLOUCESTERSHIRE

From Broad Campden to
Blockley the road climbs steeply
up Northwick Hill, over 750
feet above sea level. Across and
under the snow-covered fields to
the south-west lies the deserted
village of Upton, abandoned in
the fourteenth century.
Northwick Park nearby contains
a fine mansion, dating from the
seventeenth century, built of
Cotswold stone by the Rushout
family.

PHOTOGRAPHIC NOTES

I had visited Cleeve Hill on several occasions, and at last the weather was right. I had arrived around 3 pm and the wind was gale force. The sun was shining between black storm clouds that raced across the sky. The setting resembled rugged Scotland rather than the western Edge.

I lugged the gear up the hillside, aware that the clouds could disappear in moments, and reached my first location about halfway from the top. The wind was blowing hard, causing the tripod and camera to vibrate terribly. After a series of improvisations, the shot was eventually taken and I moved on. Within thirty minutes the day had changed completely; the sky turned deep blue, the clouds disappeared and the wind dropped.

It had taken a year to photograph the Cotswolds. After 20,000 miles of motoring and countless miles on foot, we had visited nearly every village and town in the region. We had covered an area of over 600 miles, from Hidcote Bartrim in the north to Bath in the south, from Great Tew in the east to Dursley in the west. I seldom took a photograph on the first visit; parked cars, people and the changeable British weather made sure of that. Instead, I located the best site for a shot and noted the position of the sun in anticipation of a future occasion when conditions might be better.

For the majority of the photography I was accompanied by the writer, Robin Whiteman. Having another person along can be invaluable in certain situations and Robin is now an expert at getting cars moved from an otherwise timeless scene and persuading a 'star character' to move out of the shot in order for it to be taken without people.

The photographs in this book were taken with a Nikon F3 35 mm camera, with 24, 35, 85, 180 and 300 mm Nikkor lenses. I used a polarizing filter quite frequently and the 81 series of warming filters for those occasions where their subtle usage would be beneficial. Sometimes a graduated grey filter was used to enhance the sky. The film was Kodachrome 25, during the summer months, and Fuji 50, throughout the winter. Finally, a most useful tool was a strong, steady tripod. Invariably the best ones weigh a ton – especially so on a long hike in the hills – but the steadying effect on the camera is worth the effort.

ROB TALBOT

SELECTED PROPERTIES

THE NATIONAL TRUST

Regional Information Office
The National Trust
Severn Regional Office
34–36 Church Street
Tewkesbury
Gloucestershire
GL20 5SN
Telephone: (0684) 292919/297747

Regional Information Office
The National Trust
Wessex Regional Office
Stourton
Warminster
Wiltshire
BA12 6QD
Telephone: (0747) 840560

Chedworth Roman Villa
nr. Yanworth
Cheltenham
Gloucestershire
GL54 2LJ
Telephone: (024289) 256
Open: March to end October
(Tuesday to Sunday);
November to mid December
(Wednesday to Sunday)

Dyrham Park
Chippenham
Avon
SN14 8ER
Telephone: (027582) 2501
House open: April, May & October
(daily except Thursday & Friday);
June to September (daily except Friday)
Park open: Daily

Hailes Abbey
nr. Winchcombe
Cheltenham
Gloucestershire
GL54 5PB
Telephone: (0242) 602398
Open: Daily (except at Christmas)

Hidcote Manor Garden
Hidcote Bartrim
Chipping Campden
Gloucestershire
GL55 64R
Telephone: Mickleton 333
Open: April to end October
(daily except Tuesday & Friday)

Horton Court
nr. Chipping Sodbury
Bristol
BS17 6QR
Telephone: (0454) 312653
Open: April to October
(Wednesday to Saturday)

Newark Park
Ozleworth
Wotton-under-Edge
Gloucestershire
GL12 7PZ
Telephone: (0453) 842644
Open: April, May,
August & September
(Wednesday & Thursday)

Snowshill Manor
Broadway
Worcestershire
WR12 7JU
Telephone: (0386) 852410
Open: May to September
(Wednesday to Sunday);
April & September
(Saturday & Sunday)

MISCELLANEOUS

Cotswold Farm Park
nr. Guiting Power
Cheltenham
Gloucestershire
GL54 5UG
Telephone: (04515) 307
Open: Good Friday to end September
(daily)

Roman Baths Museum
Stall Street
Bath
BA1 1IZ
Telephone: (0225) 61111
Open: Daily

Sudeley Castle
Winchcombe
Cheltenham
Gloucestershire
GL54 5JI
Telephone: (0242) 602308
Open: April to October (daily)

BIBLIOGRAPHY

Atkyns, Sir Robert, *Ancient & Present State of Glostershire*, 1712
Brill, Edith, *Cotswold Crafts*, Batsford, 1977
Brill, Edith, *Cotswold for the Curious*, Drinkwater, 1986
Brill, Edith, *Cotswold Ways*, Robert Hale, 1985
Brill, Edith, *Life & Traditions of the Cotswolds*, Dent, 1973
Brill, Edith, *Old Cotswold*, David & Charles, 1968
Brill, Edith, *Portrait of the Cotswolds*, Robert Hale, 1964
Burns, Francis, *Heigh for Cotswold: A History of Robert Dover's Olimpick Games*, Robert Dover's Games Society, 1981
Carver, Ann, *The Story of Duntisbourne Abbots*, Albert E. Smith, 1966
Carver, Ann, *The Story of Duntisbourne Rous*, Albert E. Smith, 1968
Clifford, Elsie M., *Bagendon: A Belgic Oppidum*, Heffer, 1962
Clifford, Elsie M., *Bagendon: Excavations, 1954–56*, Heffer, 1961
Cobbett, William, *Rural Rides*, 1830
Crasher, G. R., *Along the Cotswold Ways*, Cassell, 1976
Defoe, Daniel, *A Tour through the Whole Island of Great Britain*, 1724–6
Delderfield, Eric R., *The Cotswolds*, E.R.D. Publications, 1985
Derrick, Freda, *Cotswold Stone*, Chapman & Hall, 1948
Drayton, Michael (ed.), *Annalia Dubrensia: Collection of verses in honour of Dover's Hill Games & telling of their history*, 1636
Drayton, Michael, *Polyolbion*, 1613
Finberg, Josceline, *The Cotswolds*, Eyre Methuen, 1977
Gibbs, J. Arthur, *A Cotteswold Village*, Travellers' Library, 1929

Hadfield, Charles & Alice Mary, *The Cotswolds: A New Study*, David & Charles, 1973
Hadfield, Charles & Alice Mary, *Introducing the Cotswolds*, David & Charles, 1976
Hadfield, John (ed.), *The New Shell Guide to England*, Rainbird & Michael Joseph, 1981
Hammond, Reginald J. W. (ed.), *The Cotswolds*, Ward Lock, 1964
Jewson, Norman, *By Chance Did I Rove*, Earle & Ludlow, 1952
Lee, Laurie, *Cider with Rosie*, Hogarth Press, 1959
Lewis, June R., *Cotswold Villages*, Robert Hale, 1974
Lindley, E. S., *Wotton-under-Edge*, Museum Press, 1962
Massingham, H. J., *Cotswold Country*, Batsford, 1937
Massingham, H. J., *Wold Without End*, 1932
Priestley, J. B., *English Journey*, Heinemann, 1934
Rudder, Samuel, *The New History of Gloucestershire*, 1779
Rudge, Thomas, *General View of Agriculture of the County of Gloucestershire*, Board of Agriculture, 1807
Sale, Richard, *The Cotswolds*, Moorland, 1982
Sheldrick, Betty (ed.), *Cotswolds*, A.A. & Ordnance Survey, 1986
Smith, Brian, *The Cotswolds*, Batsford, 1976
Verey, David, *Gloucestershire: The Cotswolds (Buildings of England Series* ed. Nikolaus Pevsner), Penguin, 1970
Warren, C. H., *A Cotswold Year*, Bles, 1936
Witts, F. E., (ed. David Verey), *Diary of a Country Parson*, Alan Sutton, 1982
Wright, Louise, *Cotswold Heritage*, Robert Hale, 1977

INDEX

(Numbers in *Italic* refer to illustrations)